Adlerian Psychotherapy

Theories of Psychotherapy Series

Theories of Psychotherapy Series
Jon Carlson and Matt Englar-Carlson, Series Editors

Adlerian Psychotherapy

Jon Carlson and Matt Englar-Carlson

American Psychological Association

Washington, DC

Published by
American Psychological Association
750 First Street, NE
Washington, DC 20002
www.apa.org

To order
APA Order Department
P.O. Box 92984
Washington, DC 20090-2984
Tel: (800) 374-2721; Direct: (202) 336-5510
Fax: (202) 336-5502; TDD/TTY: (202) 336-6123
Online: www.apa.org/pubs/books
E-mail: order@apa.org

In the U.K., Europe, Africa, and the Middle East, copies may be ordered from
American Psychological Association
3 Henrietta Street
Covent Garden, London
WC2E 8LU England

Typeset in Minion by Circle Graphics, Inc., Columbia, MD

Printer: Maple Press, York, PA
Cover Designer: Minker Design, Sarasota, FL
Cover Art: *Lily Rising*, 2005, oil and mixed media on panel on craquelure frame, by Betsy Bauer

The opinions and statements published are the responsibility of the authors, and such opinions and statements do not necessarily represent the policies of the American Psychological Association.

Library of Congress Cataloging-in-Publication Data

Names: Carlson, Jon, author. | Englar-Carlson, Matt, author.
Title: Adlerian psychotherapy / Jon Carlson and Matt Englar-Carlson.
Description: Washington, DC : American Psychological Association, [2017] |
   Series: Theories of psychotherapy series | Includes bibliographical
   references and index.
Identifiers: LCCN 2016038830 | ISBN 9781433826597 | ISBN 1433826593
Subjects: LCSH: Adlerian psychology. | Psychotherapy.
Classification: LCC BF175.5.A33 C37 2017 | DDC 150.19/53—dc23 LC record available
at https://lccn.loc.gov/2016038830

British Library Cataloguing-in-Publication Data
A CIP record is available from the British Library.

Printed in the United States of America
First Edition

http://dx.doi.org/10.1037/0000014-000

Contents

Series Preface

Some might argue that in the contemporary clinical practice of psychotherapy, evidence-based intervention and effective outcome have overshadowed theory in importance. Maybe. But, as the editors of this series, we don't propose to take up that controversy here. We do know that psychotherapists adopt and practice according to one theory or another because their experience, and decades of good evidence, suggests that having a sound theory of psychotherapy leads to greater therapeutic success. Still, the role of theory in the helping process can be hard to explain. This narrative about solving problems helps convey theory's importance:

> Aesop tells the fable of the sun and wind having a contest to decide who was the most powerful. From above the earth, they spotted a man walking down the street, and the wind said that he bet he could get his coat off. The sun agreed to the contest. The wind blew, and the man held on tightly to his coat. The more the wind blew, the tighter he held. The sun said it was his turn. He put all of his energy into creating warm sunshine, and soon the man took off his coat.

What does a competition between the sun and the wind to remove a man's coat have to do with theories of psychotherapy? We think this deceptively simple story highlights the importance of theory as the precursor to any effective intervention—and hence to a favorable outcome. Without a guiding theory we might treat the symptom without understanding the role of the individual. Or we might create power conflicts with our clients and not understand that, at times, indirect means of helping (sunshine) are often as effective—if not more so—than direct ones (wind). In the absence of theory, we might lose track of the treatment rationale and instead get caught up in, for example, social correctness and not wanting to do something that looks too simple.

What exactly *is* theory? The *APA Dictionary of Psychology* defines theory as "a principle or body of interrelated principles that purports to explain or predict a number of interrelated phenomena." In psychotherapy, a theory is a set of principles used to explain human thought and behavior, including what causes people to change. In practice, a theory creates the goals of therapy and specifies how to pursue them. Haley (1997) noted that a theory of psychotherapy ought to be simple enough for the average therapist to understand, but comprehensive enough to account for a wide range of eventualities. Furthermore, a theory guides action toward successful outcomes while generating hope in both the therapist and client that recovery is possible.

Theory is the compass that allows psychotherapists to navigate the vast territory of clinical practice. In the same ways that navigational tools have been modified to adapt to advances in thinking and ever-expanding territories to explore, theories of psychotherapy have changed over time. The different schools of theories are commonly referred to as waves, the first wave being psychodynamic theories (i.e., Adlerian, psychoanalytic), the second wave learning theories (i.e., behavioral, cognitive-behavioral), the third wave humanistic theories (person-centered, gestalt, existential), the fourth wave feminist and multicultural theories, and the fifth wave postmodern and constructivist theories (i.e., narrative, solution-focused). In many ways, these waves represent how psychotherapy has adapted and responded to changes in psychology, society, and epistemology as well as to changes in the nature of psychotherapy itself. Psychotherapy and the theories that guide it are dynamic and responsive. The wide variety of theories is also testament to the different ways in which the same human behavior can be conceptualized (Frew & Spiegler, 2012).

It is with these two concepts in mind—the central importance of theory and the natural evolution of theoretical thinking—that we developed the APA Theories of Psychotherapy Series. Both of us are thoroughly fascinated by theory and the range of complex ideas that drive each model. As university faculty members who teach courses on the theories of psychotherapy, we wanted to create learning materials that not only highlight the essence of the major theories for professionals and professionals in training but also clearly bring the reader up to date on the current status of the models. Often in books on theory, the biography of the original theorist overshadows the evolution of the model. In contrast, our intent is to highlight the contemporary uses of the theories as well as their history and context. Further, we wanted each theory to be reflected through the process of working with clients that reflect the full range of human diversity.

As this project began, we faced two immediate decisions: which theories to address and who best to present them. We looked at graduate-level theories of psychotherapy courses to see which theories are being taught, and we explored popular scholarly books, articles, and conferences to determine which theories draw the most interest. We then developed a dream list of authors from among the best minds in contemporary theoretical practice. Each author is one of the leading proponents of that approach as well as a knowledgeable practitioner. We asked each author to review the core constructs of the theory, bring the theory into the modern sphere of clinical practice by looking at it through a context of evidence-based practice, and clearly illustrate how the theory looks in action.

There are 26 titles planned for the series. Each title can stand alone or can be put together with a few other titles to create materials for a course in psychotherapy theories. This option allows instructors to create a course featuring the approaches they believe are the most salient today. To support this end, APA Books has also developed a DVD for most of the approaches that demonstrates the theory in practice with a real client. Many of the DVDs show therapy over six sessions. Contact APA Books for a complete list of available DVD programs (http://www.apa.org/pubs/videos).

In *Adlerian Psychotherapy* we have the opportunity to share our own preferred theory of psychotherapy. This book provides what we believe is one of the first clear statements about contemporary Adlerian psychotherapy. Whereas original or classical Adlerian psychotherapy was similar to psychoanalysis as a longer term approach, the approach presented in *Adlerian Psychotherapy* is a short-term one that matches the needs and characteristics of today's clients and psychotherapists. In this contribution we offer a clear theory along with information on some of the many Adlerian techniques. We believe that most modern approaches to psychotherapy featured in the Theories of Psychotherapy Series have their roots in the Adlerian approach, whether that is clearly acknowledged or not. That awareness leads us to conclude, along with several of our Adlerian colleagues, that all therapists are probably Adlerian in some capacity; the only question is just *how* Adlerian. We hope that you will enjoy this book as much as the others in the APA Theories of Psychotherapy Series.

—Jon Carlson and Matt Englar-Carlson

REFERENCES

Frew, J., & Spiegler, M. (2012). *Contemporary psychotherapies for a diverse world* (1st Rev. Ed.). New York, NY: Routledge.

Haley, J. (1997). *Leaving home: The therapy of disturbed young people.* New York, NY: Routledge.

How to Use This Book
With APA Psychotherapy Videos

Each book in the Theories of Psychotherapy Series is specifically paired with a DVD that demonstrates the theory applied in actual therapy with a real client. Many DVDs feature the author of the book as the guest therapist, allowing students to see an eminent scholar and practitioner putting the theory they write about into action.

The DVDs have a number of features that make them excellent tools for learning more about theoretical concepts:

- Many DVDs contain six full sessions of psychotherapy over time, giving viewers a chance to see how clients respond to the application of the theory over the course of several sessions.
- Each DVD has a brief introductory discussion recapping the basic features of the theory behind the approach demonstrated. This allows viewers to review the key aspects of the approach about which they have just read.
- DVDs feature actual clients in unedited psychotherapy sessions. This provides a unique opportunity to get a sense of the look and feel of real psychotherapy, something that written case examples and transcripts sometimes cannot convey.
- There is a therapist commentary track that viewers may choose to play during the psychotherapy sessions. This track gives unique insight into why therapists do what they do in a session. Further it provides an

in vivo opportunity to see how the therapist uses the model to conceptualize the client.

The books and DVDs together make a powerful teaching tool for showing how theoretical principles affect practice. In the case of this book, the DVD *Adlerian Psychotherapy*, which features the lead author as the guest expert, provides a robust example of how this approach looks in practice.

Acknowledgments

It has been said before that if you see a turtle on top of a fence post, you know it did not get there by itself. In order for us to develop a comprehensive book on the ideas of Alfred Adler, we are grateful to the many authors, teachers, and clinicians who actively or passively guided and influenced our growth and development, shared their wisdom, and helped this book into existence. Our colleagues at Adler University and California State University, Fullerton, as well as the Adlerian community, were instrumental in providing consistent backing of our efforts. We are grateful for the support provided by Susan Reynolds and the team at APA Books. We would also like to thank the many contributors to Chapter 6 who provided their vision for the future of Adlerian psychotherapy.

I (Jon) am thankful for the relationship with my son, Matt. Early in his life I felt a certain obligation to provide the kind of fathering needed to create a healthy child. I called upon the writing of Alfred Adler for guidance. As we journeyed along the road of life things changed and I no longer needed to care for him, but instead could focus on enjoying our relationship. Today we are in a new stage of life where our roles are reversing and he is starting to look out for me. Although I have not always been conscious or aware, the journey has been a joy. I am also thankful to be able to share this journey with my wife of almost 50 years, Laura. She has been a true partner in marriage and in the Adlerian parenting of all five of our children.

I (Matt) am thankful for the relationship with my father, Jon, and the series of loving experiences and events that brought us to the point of writing a book together about Adlerian psychotherapy. My mother, Laura, had plenty to do with that as well, and I think that my ability to write and teach about Adler is the result of my parents, who provided the natural and logical consequences that helped me find my own sense of meaning and belonging. Thank you to my children, Jackson and Beatrix, for continuing the cycle and allowing my wife, Alison, and me to practice our Adlerian parenting techniques on you. Finally, thank you, Alison, for our partnership and allowing me to be in your orbit.

Adlerian Psychotherapy

1

Introduction

They may be my enemies—that I cannot help—but I will not be theirs.
—Alfred Adler

A lfred Adler wanted to help people get along with their family, friends, and others. He valued the role of cooperation with and connectedness to the world around each person (Adler, 1938; Ansbacher, 1992a; King & Shelley, 2008). His message stressed the power of personal choice; the universal fellowship of human beings; the importance of a positive, encouraging life focus; the eradication of social inequality; and the primacy of social relationships.

Alfred Adler was a pivotal figure in the history of psychotherapy. Although he originally was a colleague and early supporter of Sigmund Freud, Adler developed his own theories of the nature of humankind and soon split off from Freud to pursue these ideas (Fiebert, 1997). The split or

http://dx.doi.org/10.1037/0000014-001
Adlerian Psychotherapy, by J. Carlson and M. Englar-Carlson

disaffiliation from Freud by Adler—and later by Carl Jung—has been well documented in the history of psychology (Ellenberger, 1981; Handlbauer, 1998), as Freud, Jung, and Adler are considered the founders of modern psychotherapy. Yet it is strange to note that Freud and Jung seemed to have maintained "fame" and name recognition while Adler is not as prominent. However, Adler's ideas, unlike Freud's and Jung's, seem to be the ones that have lasted and comprise the core ingredients of most modern approaches to psychotherapy. Although his name has faded into the background, his ideas have remained at the forefront. He has become one of the most influential, yet most unacknowledged, psychologists in the field of psychotherapy.

Adler envisioned a psychology of growth, where people could strive to overcome difficulties and actually change their lives. Even though Alfred Adler inspired others (e.g., Ellis, Beck, Maslow, & Rogers) to incorporate his ideas into their emerging theories, the Adlerian approach itself has remained a comprehensive model of psychotherapy, one not well-known although the component parts seem to be everywhere.

It is fascinating to us that Adler's original ideas are consistent with the state of modern practice—even though his entire model was created nearly 100 years ago! His vision of the equality of people, encouragement, the search for what is right or positive, the emphasis on mental health and relationships, the concept of social interest, and the need to consider cultural and contextual factors are examples of cutting-edge topics with which Adler engaged to help people grow and develop their potential. Surprisingly, these ideas and many others are the bases of today's approaches to helping (Carlson, 2015a), yet there is often little reference or recognition given to Alfred Adler.

Adler's ideas are at the heart of most of the contemporary or Neo-Freudian approaches (e.g., Horney, Sullivan, & Fromm) to helping. There was actually so much similarity between the Adlerian and Neo-Freudian approaches that several scholars have suggested that these approaches should correctly be called neo-Adlerian (Mosak & Maniacci, 1999). Most of the leading contemporary psychotherapy approaches stress social relations and not just biological factors, striving for self-actualization and not being driven by the sex instinct, a subjective rather than objective approach to helping and the power of the present rather than the impact of early experiences. Adler stressed the importance of the relationship and using empathy as a key strategy for helping. His approach is at the root of cognitive behavioral, family, existential, phenomenological, schema, humanistic, and person-centered approaches (Ansbacher & Ansbacher, 1956; Bitter, 2013; Carlson, 2015a; Carlson, Watts, & Maniacci, 2006; Corey, 2016; Norcross, Hedges, & Prochaska, 2002; Watts & LaGuardia, 2015). A special issue of *The Journal of Individual Psychology* on neo-Adlerian approaches to psychotherapy will be published in 2017. The special issue will highlight the components of the leading therapy approaches that parallel Adler's theory and practice.

The individual psychology of Alfred Adler is based on a phenomenological, holistic understanding of human behavior. Adler used the term *individual psychology* for his approach in order to emphasize the indivisible (undivided or whole) nature of our personalities and refer to the essential unity of the individual psyche. Adlerians focus on holism and how each person moves through life, noting that one cannot understand an individual by analyzing their parts (i.e., reductionism), but all aspects of the person must be understood in relationship to the total pattern and in connection to social systems (Maniacci, Sackett-Maniacci, & Mosak, 2014). For example, you don't have to listen to the entire song before being able to state that it is by Beethoven. It is only necessary to uncover the pattern or melody to understand. The phenomenological perspective suggests that each person sees situations from a unique point of view. We live our life and "act as if" our view of the world is accurate or correct. When our views are distorted, our thinking becomes faulty, our emotions destructive, and our behavior inappropriate.

The Adlerian-trained psychotherapist believes that all behavior has a purpose and occurs in a social context, noting that one's cognitive orientation and *lifestyle* (literally one's style of dealing with life) is created in the first few years of life and molded within the initial social setting, the family constellation. The family constellation, including family atmosphere, family values, and gender lines, proposes that your basic birth order (psychological, not ordinal) in the family emphasizes different worldviews and life demands in order to belong within the family system. This position in your family influences your lifestyle. Each person is unique, and their style of life (i.e., lifestyle) is formed partly by seeing how other family members react to different behaviors and attitudes and partly from conclusions drawn as a child. The lifestyle is the characteristic way that we act, think, and perceive and the way we live. It is from the lifestyle that we select the methods for coping with life's challenges and tasks.

As mentioned previously, Adlerians understand all behavior as goal-directed. People continually strive to attain in the future what they believe is important or significant. Adler believed that for all people there are three basic life tasks: work, friendship, and love or intimacy. The work task is realized when work is meaningful and satisfying. The friendship task is achieved through satisfying relationships with others. The love or intimacy task is addressed by learning to love oneself as well as another. Contemporary Adlerian theorists have outlined three additional tasks, suggesting a need to master the recreational and spiritual tasks of life (Maniacci et al., 2014) as well as the task of parenting and the family (Dinkmeyer, Dinkmeyer, & Sperry, 1987). Mentally healthy people strive to master each of these tasks, which ultimately represent the challenges of life.

Adlerian theory purports that humans are social beings and therefore all behavior is socially embedded and has social meaning (Watts, 2000b). Adler emphasized the importance of relationships and being connected to others, including the larger community in which people reside. People are viewed as always trying to belong and fit into the social milieu. The outside world shapes their consciousness, as does the world of the family. A hallmark of Adlerian theory is the emphasis on *social interest*, which is a feeling of cooperation with people, the sense of belonging to and participating in the common good. Social interest can be equated with empathy and compassion for others. Adlerians value social interest to the extent that it is viewed as a measure of mental health, noting that as social interest develops, feelings of inferiority and destructive behaviors decrease (Ansbacher, 1991, 1992b; Bickhard & Ford, 1991). Adler's aim was the development of a philosophy of living that would produce a democratic family structure and a healthy social interest resulting in an ideal culture for child development (Dufrene, 2011).

Social inequality, in Adler's view, is a disease that harms entire populations. He was one of the leading advocates for the rights of women, children, and other groups marginalized by their social context. Adler promoted equal pay for women in the workplace, addressed issues of violence against women in society, and more generally promoted social equality as a mechanism for improved psychological functioning (Bitter, Robertson, Healey, & Jones-Cole, 2009). He was well aware that the health of the powerful and the marginalized were connected and that the duality of oppression meant that all people suffer in the face of social inequality. His ideas would parallel those of contemporary psychologist Daniel Goleman (2015), who has promoted the importance of emotional, social, and ecological intelligence. Goleman, like Adler, understands that happiness and satisfaction in life are results of our relationships to self, others, work, and the environment. Recently, Goleman has partnered with the Nobel Peace Prize winner, His Holiness the Dalai Lama, to emphasize the importance of compassion and social interest. Their views also parallel those of Adler's social interest, also called *Gemeinschaftsgefühl*, or community focus. Adlerian theory is designed to provide opportunities for an individual's psychological health to flourish in a community where social equality prevails. It introduces the possibility of creating a society in which psychopathology is not only treatable but also preventable (Dufrene, 2011).

Adlerians understand the individual within their social context. Therefore, the Adlerian is interested in the impact of culture and contextual factors on the individual. This contextual understanding is so embedded in the essence of the approach that those who study Adler's theory often miss it. Carlson and Sperry (1998), as well as Watts (2003), attempted to emphasize this aspect when they wrote about how Adler was one of the originators of the constructivist approach. The community, for example, was easy to see in Adler's early writings. He wrote about how circus performers as freaks of society were marginalized and ostracized, and how those working in the tailoring industry became blind from a poor work environment. Thus, the environment and the context of that environment influence the health of the individual. Later in his career Adler became focused on how people were being affected by social unrest, the wars, and the anti-Semitism/ethnic conflict/nationalism in Europe (Hoffman, 1994).

Adler also understood the many cultural differences of Europe as he attempted to deal with problems of misunderstanding between warring nations. Adler contended that so much strife and suffering could be avoided through a sound education. He saw many countries trying to work out their psychological issues, such as feelings of inferiority or insignificance, and lack of attention, through war (Bottome, 1939).

Adlerians espouse a growth model, noting that one's fate is never fixed or predetermined and that individuals are always in the process of "becoming." The Adlerian psychotherapist believes that the person who is experiencing difficulties in living, or "psychopathology," is not sick, but discouraged (Maniacci et al., 2014; Sperry, Carlson, Sauerheber, & Sperry, 2015). The Adlerian psychotherapist also views their clients as capable of using their creativity to choose alternative methods of dealing with life. Psychopathology is understood as based in mistaken notions and faulty assumptions, low social interest, discouragement, and ineffective lifestyle (Sperry et al., 2015). The task of counseling and psychotherapy then becomes one of encouraging the client to develop more social interest and create a more effective lifestyle in order to master the tasks of life.

In practice, Adlerian psychotherapy is a psychoeducational, present/future-oriented, and brief approach (Carlson, Watts, & Maniacci, 2006). Though classic Adlerian psychotherapy, which is akin to long-term psychoanalysis, is still practiced in some circles, this book focuses on a modern and contemporary approach of Adlerian psychotherapy that is consistent with other approaches that are more time-limited. Adlerian ideas and methods have been effectively applied across the full range of settings (e.g., community agencies, schools, business, child guidance centers, hospitals/medical centers, prisons, homes, private practice). The theory has been characterized as "commonsense" or "blue collar," yet it is still not commonly practiced as Adler intended and modeled. While the fundamental principles of Adlerian psychology have remained the same, new techniques and applications continue to arise, and the theory continues to evolve into the 21st century.

As one will discover when reading other books in the *Theories of Psychotherapy Series*, Adler's original ideas serve as a foundation for most modern theories of counseling and psychotherapy. Most of today's prominent theories of psychotherapy, including person-centered therapy, existential therapy, cognitive therapy, rational emotive behavioral therapy, logotherapy, strategic therapy, constructivist therapy, positive psychology, and family therapy, can find their roots in Adlerian ideas (Carlson et al., 2006; DeRobertis, 2011; Watts, 1998, 2000b, 2012; Watts & Critelli, 1997; Watts & LaGuardia, 2015; Watts & Phillips, 2004). Adlerian theory espouses a philosophy of human relations based upon social equality and emphasizes the influence of contextual factors. Further, as a psychoeducational model, Adlerian ideas can be applied in individual, group, couples, and family counseling as well as in the classroom and at the community level. As such, Adlerian theory is uniquely positioned as a complete and effective approach to meet the expanding needs of diverse clients across multiple settings (Carlson & Englar-Carlson, 2012). We believe that therapists should not ask themselves if they are an Adlerian, but just "how" Adlerian they really are.

This book provides a comprehensive review of modern Adlerian psychotherapy. In the next chapter, we describe the historical tenets of the Adlerian approach as a means of providing the foundation for better understanding of the theory (Chapter 3) and the therapeutic process of Adlerian therapy (Chapter 4). These chapters highlight the process and practice of this approach, including a variety of case examples. The fifth and sixth chapters look at the research support and the future direction of this important approach. Finally, a short summary, appendix, glossary, and suggestions for further study are provided.

2

History

The only normal people are the ones you don't know very well.

—Alfred Adler

Alfred Adler was a physician, educator, best-selling author, and a practical philosopher as well as the founding father of individual psychology. Although he was trained as a physician, he became best known as a psychologist and educator, as well as an early pro-feminist and skilled public speaker. At the roots of Adler's approach to psychotherapy were his beliefs in personal freedom, social responsibility, and the rights of children, women, and workers. While Adler was alive, he was one of the most well-known and famous psychologists. He was even more popular than Sigmund Freud, though over time Freud's fame has far surpassed Adler's. For example, his first book of popular psychology, *Understanding Human Nature*, was a huge success, selling over 100,000 copies in the first

http://dx.doi.org/10.1037/0000014-002
Adlerian Psychotherapy, by J. Carlson and M. Englar-Carlson

6 months. This is in contrast to Freud's best-selling book of the time, *The Interpretation of Dreams*, which sold around 17,000 copies over a 10-year period. Today, Freud is largely viewed as the founder of modern psychotherapy (Engel, 2008), yet there is a growing appreciation and understanding of the vast influence Adler's theories and practice has had on modern psychotherapy and counseling.

Adler's psychological and developmental concepts, such as the inferiority complex, power trips, compensation, power conflicts, control, life tasks, lifestyle, goal-oriented behavior, and social interest, have all entered the common lexicon. Professionally, Adler's theories and insights into the human personality serve as the foundation of today's most prominent theories of psychotherapy, including person-centered therapy, existential therapy, cognitive therapy, rational emotive behavioral therapy, solution-focused therapy, strategic therapy, constructivist therapy, multicultural therapy, family therapy, and even positive psychology. Almost every school of psychotherapy can trace some of its lineage back to Adler's original ideas. In many ways, Adler could be considered the grandfather of modern psychotherapy. As with many other theories, one of the best ways to understand the approach is to review how the theory was developed in light of the life of the original theorist.

THE LIFE OF ALFRED ADLER

Alfred Adler, the second of six children, was born on February 7, 1870, near Vienna, Austria. His parents were Jewish, and his father worked as a corn trader. An unhealthy child, Alfred was subject to bouts of illness, including a respiratory disorder, vitamin deficiency, and rickets, and almost died from pneumonia at the age of 4. If this was not enough, he was run over twice on the Vienna streets by horse-drawn carriages. Academically, Adler struggled in school, was required to repeat a grade level, and it was recommended that he stop formal schooling and enter a trade as an apprentice in the tailoring industry. These early experiences with feeling helpless and physically weak must have led Adler to think about a person's internal sense of inferiority or superiority.

Despite these many challenges, Alfred Adler was a happy child, who had lots of friends (Bottome, 1939). A large field was located next to his family home, and Adler would spend many hours playing with and relating to the other kids. He was well liked, had an engaging personality, and got along with other children. This was to be a pattern that continued throughout his life. He had many friends and followers and always found time to meet with them for walks or for discussions in the Vienna coffeehouses.

Generally, Adler had some discouraging experiences as a child (Hoffman, 1994). However, these experiences help to explain how he ended up compensating for his own early health and educational problems by working hard enough to gain entrance to medical school and ultimately becoming a physician. These difficult early experiences, coupled with his father's encouragement, served as catalysts that moved Adler toward studying medicine in order to fight suffering and disease. At medical school he studied ophthalmology and then neurology. It is not surprising that, before studying neurology, he would be interested in perception and how one views the world. He gained early medical experience working without pay at the *Poliklinik*, a free medical clinic that served the poor. He was also drafted for two tours of military service.

ADLER'S CONTEXTUAL AND HUMANE FOCUS

Adler's life must be understood within the sociopolitical reality of Europe during his lifetime. Although he was educated and well-known, he endured many personal and professional hardships, not to mention discrimination due to his Jewish and Hungarian heritage. Adler lived during a time when Europe was experiencing debate about competing political and social ideologies, ethnic and cultural conflicts, and long-standing historical rivalries, all of which contributed to World Wars I and II. At the end of the 18th century in Europe, one of the prevailing political ideologies was nationalism, and there was little room for those of Jewish origin within that movement. Although he was not a devout Jew (he actually converted to Christianity later in life), Adler experienced anti-Semitism and marginalization. This treatment undoubtedly informed his beliefs around the need to understand individuals in concert with the cultural context in which they lived their lives. Based on his own lived experience, he began to look for political ideologies that were more in line with his beliefs in the notions of belonging and cooperation. As a medical student Adler became interested in philosophy and politics and was drawn toward the socialism of Karl Marx. Although Adler was a proclaimed socialist in his earlier days, he turned toward the realms of existentialism and metaphysics in his later years (King & Shelley, 2008).

Alfred Adler was concerned with patient welfare and treatment. He was upset because he could not save or help many of the medical patients he treated. He was also dismayed with the research-focused medical community that seemed to care more about establishing effective diagnosis and classifying disorder and less about saving a patient's life. He was concerned about the doctor–patient relationship and believed that it was an important part of the healing process. A resurgence of this is being seen today with the increased professional interest in and importance placed on the treatment alliance and being present and mindful with clients and patients (Bottome, 1939; Hoffman, 1994).

As a socialist, Adler was less interested in economics and more intrigued by the ways that people found to fit into society and the effect society had on individuals. As a precursor to community psychology, he became active in the labor movement advocating on behalf of safe working conditions for the working poor. Adler's first book, *Health Book for the Tailoring Trade*, criticized the labor and living conditions of tailoring workers and their families. Adler also suggested improved housing and placing a limit on the number of work hours allowed during the week.

More than just theory, Adler's observations came from his own clinical experiences. He opened his first medical practice specializing in nervous diseases. Most of his medical practice was with working-class people. This differs from many of the other contemporary approaches to psychotherapy that were developed in university counseling centers or clinics with wealthier and privileged clientele (Engel, 2008). Interestingly, many of Adler's patients were circus performers, who seemed to serve as an impetus for his theory of organ inferiority (Adler, 1917). This theory suggests that people born with certain deficits develop feelings of inferiority and attempt to compensate for their real or perceived weaknesses. For example, someone with impaired hearing may become a musician or someone with weak eyesight may become a photographer.

At this time Adler was interested in psychiatry, as he believed that physicians needed to know about a patient's psychological and social state in order to treat the physical state.

Adler married Raissa Timofeivna Epstein in 1897, and she clearly had a major influence on his life (Balla, 2003; Santiago-Valles, 2009). Hoffman (1994) noted that Raissa was a strong thinker in her own right as a socialist and early feminist and that she maintained her political activities throughout her marriage. Among her friends were Leon and Natalia Trotsky, who soon became close family friends. Raissa, her friends, and the socialist-intellectual circles in Vienna had considerable influence on Adler's ideas for the rest of his life.

Yet when one looks at Adler, he was actually more of a humanist than a socialist. Adler was focused on the relationships, both familial and societal, that could be created in a community of equals. Whereas he supported socialist ideas to improve the living conditions of the poor, he also believed in the potential within individuals to change their own life. He believed education and skill training, rather than revolution, would make it possible for people to solve their problems and live life in a more satisfying fashion. He had a passionate concern for the common person and was against all forms of prejudice (Carlson, Watts, & Maniacci, 2006). Adler was also an avid supporter of women's rights and a lay movement of parent education, and strenuously argued for social belonging and community-based prevention (King & Shelley, 2008).

ADLER AND FREUD

Much has been made of the meeting between Adler and Freud in 1902, their time spent in the Psychoanalytic Society, and their subsequent acrimonious parting in 1911 (Handlbauer, 1998). In 1900, Adler wrote a strong defense of Freud's *Interpretation of Dreams*, and later Freud invited Adler to be the fifth member of his Wednesday night psychoanalytic circle

(Mosak & Maniacci, 1999). By this time, Adler was already established in his own right and thus viewed himself as more of a colleague than a student of Freud's.

Adler's relationship with Freud lasted 10 years before their parting. Their separation highlighted the stark differences in these two men in terms of their own development and approach to treatment. Whereas Freud was primarily concerned with the biological factors and psychosexual development that influence a person's behavior, Adler took a holistic perspective. Freud was deterministic in his thinking, but Adler viewed people as essentially goal directed with the capacity for being creative and responsible for their own choices. During this time Adler began to further develop his own ideas about organ inferiority, masculine protest and gender socialization, and aggression. His views were divergent from Freud's in that Adler placed more emphasis on social, familial, and cultural forces than on biological drives. He also placed less emphasis on the role of unconscious, infantile sexuality, and triumphed social drives over sexual ones (Carlson, 2015a).

Personally, the engaging and pragmatic Adler was different from the aloof and scholarly Freud. Adler did not isolate his work from the larger social and political issues of the time. His client base, unlike Freud's, consisted mostly of poor and working-class people, a group that could only prioritize "ego" strengthening as a secondary approach since, due to finances, they could not afford long-term analysis (King & Shelley, 2008). He was a man of the people and not an intellectual elite. Adler was a complex thinker who was able to distil common, pragmatic themes and write about them for the lay public in uncomplicated terms and simple language (Kurt Adler in his foreword to Hoffman, 1994). His aim was to empower others with the insightful ideas psychology had garnered (King & Shelley, 2008). Perhaps the central difference between the two men was that Adler believed that we should love our neighbor, whereas Freud asked, "Why would you want to love thy neighbor?" (Orgler, 1939/1963, p. 8). Freud also seemed to be more interested in what was best for the individual while Adler was concerned with what was best for the other or mankind.

In 1911, when Adler was the president of the Psychoanalytic Society, the growing differences became too much, and Adler and Freud parted ways. Although a reconciliation was attempted, it failed. Adler, along with one third of the members of the Psychoanalytic Society, went on to form what became The Society for Individual Psychology. This was a significant moment in the history of psychotherapy because an alternative school of thought was established that acknowledged the influence of biological factors but stressed the social and cultural influences on personality so popular in today's approaches to helping. Further, due to Adler's own experiences working with "common" people, his model emphasized ethical and practical solutions (Bankart, 1997). Interestingly, Adler's century-old ideas about equity and humanity are compatible with the current ethical guidelines of both the American Psychological Association and the American Counseling Association that relate to treatment with regard to race, gender, ethnicity, social class, and sexual orientation (Carlson et al., 2006).

ESTABLISHING THE ADLERIAN APPROACH

Adler went on to serve as a doctor in World War I and then established 30 child-guidance clinics in Austria that were staffed by volunteer psychologists. In these community-based clinics he would counsel families live on a stage in front of an audience. Adler believed that problems were *universal*, meaning that families have many common problems due to the societal change that was creating a shift from autocratic to democratic living. Therefore, he could use the problems of the family on stage to teach the entire audience how to approach and resolve the problems in their own families as a form of *spectator therapy*. He also became active in school reform, child-rearing practices, and public family education.

Adler escaped his homeland just prior to the outbreak of Nazi domination and immigrated to the United States in 1935. For many years before his immigration, Adler and his ideas were becoming well-known in the United States in both public and professional circles. During this time, Adler was one of the premier lecturers and authors worldwide, but particularly in the United States. Writing in a simple, practical, and nontechnical style, Adler taught people to recognize how negative behavior could limit their lives and provided outlines on how to change and improve the quality of life.

Adler believed that people needed training in how to live life as equals. He believed this training could occur through the written and spoken word, and not just through therapy. During his lectures he would also provide live demonstrations of parenting techniques to crowds of thousands.

Back issues of newspapers from the 1920s and 1930s from around the United States highlight Adler's messages. In newspaper articles, he is frequently quoted talking about the importance of not pampering children and urging parents to not do things for their children that they can do for themselves. He asserted that women and men were equal and that people were better motivated by encouragement than by threats of harm or punishment. His tips and suggestions were sought after and devoured in a country that was struggling between World Wars and a recent financial upheaval that had changed feast to famine. Adler seemed to serve as a guiding light, helping people to move closer to a life of happiness and personal satisfaction.

The social movement from autocratic to democratic living was occurring, and Adler found himself at the forefront with his own liberal views as well as the revolutionary ideas of his wife and friends. He realized that people had been raised in a hierarchical system and therefore needed skills to learn to live as equals. Although many believed in the concepts and ideals of democracy, they did not know how to treat one another in a democratic or equal fashion. Men talked down to women, adults to children, bosses to employees, rich to poor, not to mention the difference between people along ethnic, racial, and religious lines. To make a difference, Adler concentrated on helping parents and teachers educate children effectively. He believed that by changing these basic relationships it would be possible to eventually change the entire society.

Adler chose New York as the base for his clinical and lecturing activities, and he spent the latter part of his life promoting his theory, eventually recruiting others (Ansbacher & Ansbacher, 1956; Dreikurs, 1967) to carry on his work. Adler and Raissa had four children. Kurt and Alexandra followed their father into psychiatry/psychotherapy and practiced in New York City for many years. Cornelia, the middle child, was an artist. The eldest daughter, Valentine, was politically and socially active like Raissa.

It was reported that she and her husband perished in a Russian gulag just prior to Adler's death. Many speculated that his heart was broken when he heard of her death (Hoffman, 1994). Alfred Adler died shortly thereafter of a heart attack while walking on the streets of Aberdeen, Scotland, on a lecture tour in 1937.

At the time of his death, Adler was very well-known in the Western world. There was only one grandchild, Kurt's daughter Margot Adler, who was a well-known social activist and reporter for National Public Radio until her early death in 2014.

ADLER'S LEGACY AND ADVANCEMENT OF INDIVIDUAL PSYCHOLOGY

Adler's early writings up until and during World War I focused primarily on abnormal human behavior and were psychoanalytic in tone. However, following World War I, Adler became more interested in normal human behavior and progressively developed his mature theory, which is more holistic, phenomenological, and socially oriented than psychoanalytic theory (Slavik & Carlson, 2006). Contemporary Adlerian psychology and psychotherapy is primarily based on Adler's later period and subsequent developments by later Adlerians (e.g., Rudolf Dreikurs, Heinz and Rowena Ansbacher, Don Dinkmeyer, Harold Mosak, Mim Pew, Bernard Shulman, Bob Powers, Jane Griffiths, Edna Nash, Manford Sonstegard, Jon Carlson, Judy Sutherland, Julia Yang, Len Sperry, James Bitter, Betty Lou Bettner, Michael Maniacci, Eva Ferguson Dreikurs, Leigh Johnson-Migalski, Terry Kottman, Roy Kern, Susan Belangee, Richard Watts, Marion Balla, and Mary Francis Schneider), who evolved the approach to match contemporary modes of practice.

Adler was not only ahead of his time but also limited by the historical era in which he lived. Kottler (2002) noted that many of Adler's important contributions to current practice might seem rather obvious because they have formed the bases of so many other theories. Prochaska and Norcross (2010) stated that many of "Adler's ideas have quietly permeated modern psychological thinking, often without notice. It would not be easy to find another author from which so much has been borrowed from all sides without acknowledgment than Alfred Adler" (p. 91). As a psychotherapist, Adler was the first to introduce the importance of thinking processes on feelings; the impact of early family experiences and birth order on present behavior; the value of constructing specific plans of action; the building of an egalitarian, collaborative counseling relationship (including having the client and counselor face each other); an assessment of lifestyle and social behavior as they affect personality development; the importance of skill training; and an educational model of treatment. As we previously mentioned, Adler also became quite involved in the social rights and social justice movements of his day, advocating for school reform and sex education, and being a vocal leader in equal rights for women. Adler wanted to be a humble and modest man and wrote of his efforts to expunge arrogance from his character (Adler, 1929). He would rather his theories survive than have people remember his name (Mosak, 2005).

Rudolf Dreikurs founded the first Adler Institute in Chicago as a way to introduce Adler's ideas to emerging psychology professionals, who primarily knew traditional psychoanalytic thinking. Adler's children, Kurt and Alexandra, created a similar center in New York City. Each of these training institutes nurtured the growth of Adlerian psychology at a time when the dominance of Freudian ideas made this difficult. This was particularly challenging because Adler was often branded as a traitor to Freud's original teachings. Although Adler did indeed directly contradict the orthodoxy of Freudian theory, he was consistent in crediting Freud with promoting the role of early-childhood experiences, bringing attention to the meaning of dreams, and suggesting that symptoms served some useful purpose (Mosak & Maniacci, 1999). Dreikurs shared Adler's vision of child-guidance centers and went on to make a considerable impact with his books on child rearing, *Children: The Challenge* (Dreikurs & Soltz, 1964) and *Discipline Without Tears* (Dreikurs & Cassell, 1972). Dreikurs was also instrumental in popularizing Adlerian principles in the education system and wrote *Psychology in the Classroom* (Dreikurs, 1958) and *Encouraging Children to Learn* (Dinkmeyer & Dreikurs, 1963). These Adlerian principles included encouragement, individual responsibility, democratic rules, social awareness, and the use of natural and logical consequences rather than punishment (Pryor & Tollerud, 1999). These ideas continued to gain a stronger foothold in parenting education, as they became the basis for many of the more popular parenting curriculums such as the evidence-based programs *Active Parenting* and *Systematic Training for Effective Parenting* (Lindquist & Watkins, 2014).

THE PROGRESSION OF THE ADLERIAN APPROACH

When Dreikurs died in 1972, the Adlerian movement lacked a charismatic spokesperson to continue advancing the theory in both the public and the academic sectors. There were many competent modern Adlerians, such as Don Dinkmeyer, Harold Mosak, Bernard Shulman, and Robert Powers, but there was no one person that could unify the Adlerians like Alfred Adler and Rudolf Dreikurs. This was a time when Adlerians were confused between adhering to the original words and theories of Adler and Dreikurs for direction, or picking up where they left off by continuing to adapt and advance the approach in accordance with modern therapeutic practice and mental health trends.

In many ways, the question of the relevancy of Adlerian ideas in modern times reflected the struggle that many Adlerians have faced over the past 30 years of figuring out who they wanted to be. Among Adlerians, questions remained as to whether Adlerian psychotherapy needed to become contemporary and adapt to address current problems or to follow the classical guidelines of the founders. This struggle was highlighted by a call for Adlerians to develop strategies and ideas to go "on beyond Adler" (Carlson, 1989). Carlson (1989) noted,

> Adler's/Dreikurs's original ideas had considerable promise for humankind, but they were only beginnings, not final and finite principles. It is as if Adlerians live in the world of the 1920s, a world that Adler understood so well . . . it is important to modify Adlerian ideas to apply to today's tough issues, issues that did not exist in the 1920s. (p. 411)

A decade later, Carlson (2000) posed a question to Adlerians, asking who they wanted to be in the contemporary psychotherapy world, an "Astronaut or Dinosaur? Headline or Footnote?" (p. 3). This challenge was offered in the context of modern psychotherapy and counseling that in many ways has moved away from allegiance to single theories of personality and change and has readily adopted integrative theoretical models. The solution for Adlerians today is a combination of recognizing the wisdom and vision of Adler's original ideas while continuing to adapt and evolve the application of the theory to modern practice and societal concerns.

In recent years, it seems that most Adlerians have chosen to become a continued presence in contemporary psychotherapy. Adler's theory of individual psychology is enjoying tremendous popularity as many writers have adapted the original theory to a variety of other applications and settings, each of which brings the original ideas into a fresh package (see Carlson & Slavik, 1997; Carlson et al., 2006; Dinkmeyer & Sperry, 2000; Mosak & Maniacci, 1998, 1999; Sonstegard, Bitter, & Pelonis, 2004; Sperry & Carlson, 2013; Sperry, Carlson, Sauerheber, & Sperry, 2015; Stein, 2013; Watts, 2003; Watts & Carlson, 1999; Yang & Milliren, 2009). *The Journal of Individual Psychology* has many articles showing how Adler's ideas can be used in treating a wide variety of clients and problems in numerous settings. Further, authors have explored how Adlerian theory can be used to support clients of various racial and ethnic groups (Carlson & Carlson, 2000; Chung & Bemak, 1998; Herring & Runion, 1994; Kawulich & Curlette, 1998; Moore & McDowell, 2014; Perkins-Dock, 2005; Reddy & Hanna, 1995; Roberts, Harper, Caldwell, & Decora, 2003; Roberts, Harper, Tuttle Eagle Bull, & Heideman-Provost, 1998; Sapp, 2014), spiritual and religious backgrounds (Baruth & Manning, 1987; Cheston, 2000; Ecrement & Zarski, 1987; Ellis, 2000; Johansen, 2005; Kanz, 2001; Mansager, 2000; Mansager et al., 2002; Noda, 2000; Sauerheber & Bitter, 2013; Watts, 2000a), internationally (see two special issues of *The Journal of Individual Psychology*, Volume 68, 3 and 4) and other marginalized groups (Chandler, 1995; Hanna, 1998; Matteson, 1995; Shelley, 2009; Suprina, Brack, Chang, & Kim, 2010). Adlerians have published works to show how to work with families, couples, children, and groups across all treatment settings. The techniques and theory have been clearly described. Keep in mind, though, a few professionals, such as Henry Stein of the Alfred Adler Institute of Northwestern

Washington, still practice "classical" Adlerian therapy today. This approach is long-term treatment that is similar to psychoanalysis and is the form of Adlerian psychotherapy practiced in many European countries.

One of the ways that Adlerians have remained contemporary is by recognizing how aspects of Adler's original model are theoretically consistent with modern psychotherapy needs and expectations. Adlerian psychotherapy is a psychoeducational, present/future-oriented, and time-limited (or brief) approach (Carlson et al., 2006; Corey, 2016; Watts, 2000b). Clearly, Adlerian psychotherapy fits well within the contemporary integrative zeitgeist of psychotherapy. As Dinkmeyer and Sperry (2000) indicated, "there is increasing interest in emphasizing the commonalities and converging themes among psychotherapy systems" (p. 9), and psychotherapy integration is the prevalent focus among many psychotherapy theorists, researchers, and practitioners. Adlerian therapy is both integrative and eclectic, clearly blending cognitive, psychodynamic, and systemic perspectives while having considerable common ground with postmodern approaches such as constructivist, solution-focused, and narrative therapies (Watts, 2000b; Watts & LaGuardia, 2015). As a relational and constructivist psychology, Adlerian therapy affirms that humans cannot be understood apart from their social context and the relationships therein. Adlerian therapy inclusively affirms both the collectivistic and individualistic aspects of human functioning. The Adlerian view of humankind is "a healthy balance of the individual rooted in relationships" (Jones & Butman, 1991, p. 237).

Most important, for any approach to be considered a relevant psychotherapy for contemporary society, it must successfully address multicultural and social equality issues (Comas-Díaz, 2014). It is significant that Adler developed his original theories and model while campaigning for the social equality of women, contributing to the understanding of gender issues, speaking out for the rights of working-class and poor people, and addressing the rights of minority groups. Within that context, many practitioners of Adlerian therapy were addressing social equality and understanding of people within a contextual framework long before multiculturalism became a dominant force in counseling and psychotherapy (Watts, 2000b). Arciniega and Newlon (1999) noted that the characteristics and assumptions of Adlerian psychology are congruent with the cultural values of many minority racial and ethnic groups and affirmed that the Adlerian therapeutic process is respectful of cultural diversity.

In their continuing efforts to train students to be socially focused and responsible practitioners, the Adler University in Chicago has based their curriculum on the concept of social interest or community engagement in order to further highlight the importance of addressing the larger social issues such as poverty, violence, and discrimination. Each student who attends Adler University must complete a 200-hour social justice practicum in each of their training years. It appears that Adlerian therapy is alive, well, and poised to address the concerns of a contemporary global society. As Mosak (2005) noted, "The Adlerian is not interested in curing sick individuals or a sick society, but in reeducating individuals and in reshaping society" (p. 63).

The next chapter discusses how Adlerians have addressed the evolution of a modern Adlerian theory.

3

Theory

By changing our opinion of ourselves we can also change ourselves.

—Alfred Adler

This chapter highlights the concepts that provide the foundation for how an Adlerian therapist understands human personality and conceptualizes a client's concerns. The theoretical guidelines provide the Adlerian therapist with a checklist of those areas that are most critical in their work with clients.

Alfred Adler highlighted the importance the social and cultural contexts hold for the development of the personality. He believed that people create their own beliefs about themselves and the world. Some beliefs are accurate, while others are inaccurate or faulty. Adler believed that these inaccurate/faulty beliefs were formed early in life through interpretations of early experiences and perpetuated by living life as though these beliefs

http://dx.doi.org/10.1037/0000014-003
Adlerian Psychotherapy, by J. Carlson and M. Englar-Carlson

were accurate. Faulty beliefs develop from the way the individual perceives early life experiences. The family life/constellation, birth order, socio-economic status, political climate, contextual forces, and so on, all impact the conclusions one reaches. The role of the Adlerian therapist is to help the client to become aware of their faulty worldview and to educate them into a healthier one resulting in corresponding changes in feelings and behavior.

GOALS OF ADLERIAN PSYCHOTHERAPY

The major goal of the Adlerian therapist is to increase or foster the client's social interest and community feeling. Milliren, Evans, and Newbauer (2007) identified the goal of Adlerian therapy as "assist[ing] clients to understand their unique lifestyles . . . and to act in such a way as to meet the tasks of life with courage and social interest" (p. 145). Adler (1927a) added, "to be of any help you must change the whole attitude to life of the individual. So long as the patient persists in his morbid attitude, you cannot get rid of the symptoms" (p. 6).

The other goals include all of the following:

- To help the client to like who they are and to encourage equality and belonging in a positive manner.
- To help the client positively address the tasks of life.
- To create positive and satisfying relationships with others, including the significant people in the client's life (i.e., partner, children, siblings, parents, friends, bosses, colleagues).
- To obtain satisfying work and become a contributing member of the world community.
- To understand the spiritual dimension, addressing questions such as the meaning of life, why I am here, and how I can leave a legacy.
- To be able to have fun and look at life in a manner indicative of someone who is happy and possesses a sense of humor.
- To learn maintenance skills in order to learn and grow.
- To reduce discouragement and feelings of inferiority, which will often result in removing the presenting problem or symptom.

These goals provide the guidelines for the Adlerian therapist to understand what is important in the client's presentation. Assessment in each of these areas occurs in order to understand the client's strengths and to determine areas for intervention. The therapist collaborates with the client to create a treatment plan that indicates what aspects are most important. Each client is unique, and the Adlerian therapist realizes that the treatment plan should respect both the problem the client wants help with and the degree to which they want assistance.

Most Adlerians view their clients as discouraged individuals and favor using a growth model that emphasizes the client's strengths. The focus in therapy is on health, well-being, and prevention of problems rather than remediation. Adlerian psychology itself provides an optimistic approach that views people as creative problem solvers who are capable and responsible, and this ethos is integrated throughout the approach. Accordingly, the client–therapist relationship is one of equals in which the therapeutic process of helping is focused on teaching, providing information, and offering encouragement (Ansbacher & Ansbacher, 1956). Encouragement is viewed as the most powerful tactic in the Adlerian therapist's arsenal. Further, Dreikurs (1971) considered the ability to encourage others as the single most important attribute in getting along with other people. The loss of courage, or discouragement, results in mistaken and dysfunctional behavior. Therefore, the therapist concentrates on changing beliefs, building self-confidence, and practicing compassion while developing courage.

KEY CONCEPTS

An Adlerian approach to psychotherapy comprises several core concepts. Each of these concepts informs how Adlerians conceptualize clients and their health.

Holism

For some, the term *individual psychology* can be misleading. Rather than emphasizing individual aspects of a person, Adler actually meant the opposite; the term *individual* was actually meant as *indivisible*. Adlerian theory proposed *holism*, which is the notion that understanding a person and their behavior necessitates a consideration of the entire field in which a person lives, namely, that "all aspects of a person connect to all other aspects of that person" (Milliren & Clemmer, 2006, p. 18). Thus, a central assumption in Adlerian psychology is that every person is unique and greater than the sum of one's parts. Adler used the term *individual psychology* to stress unity within a person and to encourage looking at people as individuals, and not as a collection of parts or part functions (e.g., id, ego, superego, drives, emotions). This is the opposite of reductionism. Therefore, all of the components that make up the personality are seen to function holistically, and to understand a person, one must understand all of the person rather than just parts.

Rather than looking at polarities (e.g., mind and body, conscious and unconscious, cognition and affect, approach and avoidance), Adlerians look at the interaction of all components and how clients put them to use. Polarities are only important as the subjective experiences of each person (Mosak, 2005). The mind and the body are viewed as an interconnected, reciprocal process that cannot be understood when separated. For example, an Adlerian would look at the *organ jargon* of each client. Organ jargon provides a framework for understanding clients who exhibit physical symptoms, whether or not the symptoms are predominantly organic or functional (Griffith, 2006). It connotes the connection between the physical, emotional, and psychological. Adler (1956) stated that "physical symptoms speak a language which is usually more expressive and discloses the individual's opinion more clearly than words are able to . . . The emotions and their physical expressions tell us how the mind is acting and reacting" (p. 223). An Adlerian might view someone with a rash as having something "under their skin" that needs to be expressed. This implies more than the physical problem, and therefore the therapist would also look into the client's relationship world. The Adlerian assumption is that a person is unified in action, thoughts, feelings, convictions, attitudes, characteristics, and so on, and all of these are expressions of uniqueness that are viewed holistically to reflect a plan in life to reach self-selected *life goals*, which are in turn viewed as beneficial to others. Furthermore, each person is connected to social systems and interpersonal relationships that interact in a systemic manner of reciprocal influence. Regardless of cultural background, each person functions as a member of groups in daily living (Miranda, Frevert, & Kern, 1998).

The clinical implication is that an Adlerian therapist will look at the "whole person" when doing an assessment. In Adlerian terms, this means exploring the client's world from a holistic perspective that takes into consideration the biological, psychological, and social factors. Dreikurs (1967) described holism as the social context each person is in. He indicated that a person cannot be understood without looking at their social context. For example, a child can only be understood by looking at one's family.

Encouragement

Encouragement is a core aspect of human development and one of the central components in Adlerian therapy. Adlerians view clients as discouraged (i.e., lacking motivation and belief in their abilities to change) rather than ill (Watts & Pietrzak, 2000); consequently, the therapist's use of encouragement—the antidote to discouragement—becomes foundational to the process of therapeutic change (Main & Boughner, 2011; Watts & Pietrzak, 2000).

Encouragement refers to the process of increasing one's courage in order to face the difficulties in life. People can be encouraged or discouraged (Ansbacher & Ansbacher, 1956; Dreikurs, 1967; Wong, 2015). If they are encouraged, people will risk doing things if it leads toward growth, and it will help people become more engaged with their community (Main & Boughner, 2011). People who are encouraged do not perceive the world as a hostile place. They are willing to risk being wrong because it is not a threat to their *self-concept* (i.e., the sum total of all of the beliefs about "who I am") and *self-ideal* (i.e., ideals about how the world and people operate; Carlson, Watts, & Maniacci, 2006). If they are discouraged, people will not risk and will become rigid with their convictions and not look for growth opportunities. For Adler and Dreikurs, psychopathology represented *discouragement*, the feeling of not belonging in the world in a useful or constructive manner. Discouragement could arise from many places, such as disturbed thoughts or adverse life circumstances and conditions (Ferguson, 2001). The way an individual views (i.e., thoughts or cognitions) circumstances is of primary interest. Adlerians are more interested in what life circumstances mean to the individual rather than what the actual life circumstances were. For example, when talking about her childhood, a client reveals that she grew up in poverty and that many nights she went to bed hungry. The therapist asked her what it was like growing up poor, and she responded, "We had lots of love and learned to make lemons out of lemonade." More objective psychologies are more concerned with what has factually happened in a person's life, whereas the Adlerian wants to also know what it means to the person. In this example, the client is living her life with courage and can see that strength in surviving her difficult childhood circumstances.

Although encouragement is at the basis of Adlerian theory it means different things to different people. Wong (2015) attempted conceptual clarity with the following definition of encouragement: "the expression of affirmation through language or other symbolic representations to instill courage, perseverance, confidence, inspiration, or hope in a person(s) within the context of addressing a challenging situation or realizing a potential" (p. 182). He went on to document the research effectiveness and the positive impact of using encouragement.

Encouragement influences how Adlerians understand people's concerns and difficulties in life. Dreikurs (1967) noted that presenting problems are based on discouragement and that without "encouragement, without having faith in himself restored, (the client) cannot see the possibility of doing or functioning better" (p. 62). Thus, discouragement from family members, parents, peers, and society can contribute to problems in life by lowering one's self-esteem and self-worth while contributing to feelings of inferiority. Adlerian therapists teach their clients that although the past cannot be changed, their attitudes about the past can. For many clients, this can be a freeing revelation because the past and their place in it can be reconfigured or re-storied in more self-fulfilling ways.

Encouragement serves as an active therapeutic stance and a technique to initiate change. Therapists with a high expectation for client improvement are positively correlated with clinically significant change in clients

(Connor & Callahan, 2015). Adler was unequivocal that therapists were to encourage through action, namely, that "hope absent of action was not a plan—nor was it accessible to clients" (Main & Boughner, 2011, p. 269). Thus, the therapist's task was to inspire "courage" in the client so that the client would take action to engage in the community and to serve others. This is similar to the stance that has recently been "discovered" in the positive psychology movement and espoused by collaborative and constructivist approaches to therapy (Watts, 2012). Adler stated that "in every step of treatment, we must not deviate from the path of encouragement" (Ansbacher & Ansbacher, 1956, p. 342). The inverse of discouragement, encouragement means to give another courage and hope. Courage occurs when clients become aware of their strengths, and at the same time they feel less alienated and alone. It is the fundamental, positive way that the Adlerian therapist looks at the client. They see the entire person beginning with their strengths and assets and then their liabilities and challenges. Encouragement is a process of focusing on a person's resources and giving positive recognition in order to build a person's self-esteem, self-concept, and self-worth (Dinkmeyer, McKay, & Dinkmeyer, 2008).

In terms of parenting, encouragement focuses on stressing the positive and letting children learn from disappointment. It means recognizing any positive movement, having positive expectations, and valuing children for who they are. Adlerians believe that all children need encouragement and that providing children self-confidence is the best way to encourage their development. Adlerians often say that "encouragement to a child is like water to a plant." Children with confidence and courage will meet whatever problem lies ahead as something coming from within which they can alter and control (Carlson et al., 2006). Pampered, overprotected, and physically sick children have their self-esteem undermined by overly helpful adults. This has to be corrected. "Don't do things for children that they can do for themselves" is a helpful rule. Otherwise, we are meaning to be helpful but unwittingly sending the nonverbal message "I don't think *you* can do this; therefore, *I* have to."

Encouragement begins with acknowledging that life can be difficult and it is necessary to instill faith in clients that they have the potential to change. Encouragement is a movement toward helping clients use all of their personal and external resources to achieve desired changes. For example, in an opening psychotherapy session, the therapist can provide the client with encouragement that, although things are difficult, change is possible. This approach builds some expectancy and conveys to the client that they can get through each of the many challenges being faced. As much as possible, the therapist adopts a positive, optimistic position to balance the often greater attention that clients give to their distressing and discouraging life problems. Encouragement also includes looking at the existing successes and positive resources available to the client. Lambert's (2013) classic research on the common factors attributes 40% of change in therapy to client factors, including the client's strengths and assets. Further, Adlerians know the difference between encouragement and praise/compliments, as the latter implies an evaluation or approval of the client as a person (e.g., "I think you did great"), and this may constitute an external source of reinforcement (Sweeney, 2009).

The emphasis on encouragement can be particularly useful and appropriate for populations that have histories and experiences of being marginalized and oppressed in the United States and elsewhere (see Wong, 2015). Many people in the United States experience constant discouragement at the individual, community, and societal levels due to prejudice and institutional discrimination associated with gender, race and ethnicity, sexual orientation, social class, and immigration status. In many ways, entire populations are discouraged, marginalized, and made to feel powerless and invisible in the United States. Within that context, the use of encouragement and acceptance can be an extremely validating and supportive process with sociopolitical ramifications for both the client and the therapist. It can build perseverance and help people remain connected through action to their communities.

Subjective or Private Logic

Adlerian therapists strive to understand the world from the client's point of view. Taking a phenomenological stance, Adlerians look at the individual or unique way that a client perceives the world. The reasoning that individuals use to justify and account for their style of life is known as *private logic.* Freud based his psychology and theories on biology and instinctual determinism. Adler thought that Freud's view was too narrow, that people are not merely determined by heredity and environment but have the capacity to interpret, influence, and create events. Heredity and environment serve as the "frame and influence" within which people work to create their lives. Ultimately, people have the capacity and choice to grow (Ansbacher & Ansbacher, 1956). Adlerian theory purports that each person creates their own reality. This process is uniquely subjective and private, rather than objective and universally agreed upon, which could be referred to as commonsense or consensual reality. Foreshadowing the development of cognitive interventions, Adler believed that any experience can have many different possible interpretations, depending on the way a person chooses to look at the situation (Carlson et al., 2006). According to Carlson and Sperry (1998), the realization that individuals coconstruct the reality in which they live and are also able to question, deconstruct, or reconstruct reality for themselves is a fundamental tenet not only of Adlerian psychotherapy but also of other constructivist psychotherapies (Watts & Phillips, 2004).

One's subjective reality includes perceptions, thoughts, beliefs, and conclusions. Adler was significantly influenced by the philosopher Hans Vaihinger's (1924) book, *The Philosophy of "As If,"* which emphasized that human cognitive processes serve a purposeful, instrumental, and functional significance for survival and activity in the world. Adler drew upon Vaihinger's work for the notion of *fictions* or subjective-thought constructs that, although not necessarily corresponding with reality, serve as useful tools for coping with the tasks and problems of living. Adler (1931/1992) noted,

> Human beings live in the realm of *meanings.* We do not experience things in the abstract; we always experience them in human terms. Even at its source our experience is qualified by our human perspective. We experience reality only through the meaning we ascribe to it: not as a thing in itself, but as something interpreted. (p. 15)

One's lifestyle is built upon deeply established personal beliefs or constructs that are referred to as private logic, composed of ideas developed in early childhood that may or may not be appropriate to later life. Simply stated, Adlerians believe that *you are what you think* (Carlson et al., 2006). When you think or focus on something, the more you see of it. As people develop and grow, ideas are formed about right and wrong based on their subjective personal experience. For example, if early experiences were painful and discouraging, one may develop mistaken ideas or *faulty logic.* This can occur when children cannot find a healthy way to feel significant within the family. Logic becomes faulty when the only way an individual behaves is to fit within the family via negative ways. To achieve some sort of significance, children may learn that the only way to get attention is to act out in ways that are negative and not useful to the group. So temper tantrums and misbehavior do the trick, as do fighting and churlishness. The private logic behind children's attention-seeking behavior is the belief that they do not count or are not important and need others to notice them in order to be somebody. If the only times they are noticed by others is when they misbehave, then misbehavior becomes their style of seeking attention and their faulty logic is cemented. Even if the attention they receive is painful, for most children, any kind of attention is better than no attention at all.

For Adlerian therapists, subjective and private logic means it is more important to understand a client's perception of past events and how this interpretation of early events has a continuing influence on the client's life. How life is, in reality, is less important to an Adlerian therapist than how an individual client believes life to be. Consider a 12-year-old boy who believes his soccer team is one of the best in the league even though they have lost each of their games by a large margin. His beliefs do not seem to be impacted by the reality of the score, but instead may be influenced by a positive self-concept and expectation that he and his team have value. A person's outlook is influenced by the cultural context from the past and present, suggesting that the meaning of any stressor is culturally based. Among other things, that meaning can come from family or societal contexts that either encourage or discourage individuals.

Lifestyle

The Adlerian construct of personality is called the *lifestyle* or style of life. Unique to each person, lifestyle is an individual's attitudinal set that

includes the basic convictions, choices, and values that influence decisions and behaviors (Ansbacher & Ansbacher, 1956; Mosak & Maniacci,
1999; Shulman & Mosak, 1988; Stein & Edwards, 1998). The lifestyle
describes the individual and that which is created collectively, which are
strongly influenced by one's cultural surroundings (Frevert & Miranda,
1998). Lifestyle is the characteristic way one moves toward life goals and
strives for superiority. Created in early childhood within a social context,
lifestyle serves as a blueprint for coping with the tasks and challenges of
life. Adler indicated that individuals could only be understood within a
social context and that the family provided the first and most important
context. The social context of childhood includes both the context of
one's culture of origin and the experiences with their *family constellation*
(Adler's term for the psycho-socio-political organization and structure of
the primary-family group). The family constellation includes attention to
birth order, the individual's perception of self, sibling characteristics, and
parental relationships. Children learn about their role within the family and see how their family and others occupy and navigate the world,
and thus tend to model their lifestyle upon these early perceptions and
relationships. In terms of multicultural considerations, Reddy and Hanna
(1995) noted that the Adlerian notion of lifestyle lends itself to the conceptualization of both the individual and the collective, which is a crucial
aspect of effective multicultural therapy. Adlerian theory then emphasizes
the influence of subjective individualized psychological processes in the
formation of lifestyle within a homogeneous description of one's culture
(Miranda & Fraser, 2002).

Children are also influenced by factors outside of the home (Powers &
Griffith, 1987). The roles of peers, school personnel, neighbors, coaches,
friends and their families, and other community and cultural institutions
need to be considered. For many children, the first significant contact with
adults other than their parents happens when they go to school and meet
teachers. These factors need to be assessed as well and often provide clues
to understanding the nuances of the lifestyle.

Adlerians believe that one's style of life is fixed at 5 or 6 years of age
(Ansbacher & Ansbacher, 1956). Because Adlerian theory is a growth
model, Adlerian therapists believe that lifestyle tends to undergo some

refinement throughout life, although for the most part the core lifestyle remains stable. One way that a person's basic convictions (i.e., the rules governing how to belong) can change is if a therapeutic event occurs. This event does not need to be actual therapy, and often it is not. For example, a man who believes he is unlovable can have a therapeutic-like conversion if he finds someone who loves him. That experience can truly change the life of the once "unlovable" one.

Numerous cultural and contextual factors also influence the development of lifestyle. Frevert and Miranda (1998) used lifestyle to conceptualize the Latino/a culture and treatment of Latinos in the United States. They noted that an important influence on the lifestyle of many Latinos is the effect of migration and immigration on psychological adjustment. For example, they noted that a fifth-generation Mexican American may be exceptionally different from a recent immigrant from El Salvador based on acculturation and extended contact with the host culture.

Lifestyle serves many purposes (Carlson et al., 2006). First, it is a guide to help a person navigate and make sense of life. Second, lifestyle is also a "limiter" of what any one individual will do or not do. For example, imagine a responsible and focused man with a mild-mannered personality. This limits the range of responses he will master and demonstrate in certain situations. If he were involved in a minor car accident, it would be out of character for him to either leave the scene of the accident or aggressively attack the other driver verbally or physically. He would not think of it or even necessarily know how to be irresponsible or violent. Third, lifestyle provides security and a sort of rhythm to life. In the process of meaning making and value creating, structure and guidance are required, but predictability and regularity are also necessary. Our lifestyle allows us to develop habits—in other words, habitual responses that do not need cortical control; that is, we do not have to think about it, we just respond to events in our habitual or "automatic" way. Thus, the lifestyle can be viewed as the overarching set of rules (i.e., "rules of the road") for how humans prepare themselves for life's contingencies (Mosak & Maniacci, 1999).

Lifestyle also helps explain how our behaviors fit together so that there is a consistency to our actions. No two people have an identical lifestyle, as each person develops different talents that consist of a subjective view about oneself and the world. Since Adlerian therapists believe that all behavior is goal directed, once they understand a client's lifestyle they can begin to make sense of the client's experiences, or at the very least, help the client to develop this for themself.

Another way to understand lifestyle is to look at how an individual approaches the life tasks of love, friendship, and work. It goes without saying that not all lifestyles are effective all the time in successfully accomplishing life tasks.

For Adlerian therapists, emotions serve the lifestyle, they do not interfere with it (Dreikurs, 1967). People do not experience emotions that disrupt their styles; rather, they create emotions in order to facilitate their styles. Like behavior, all emotions serve a purpose, and by knowing the lifestyle, a therapist can see how the emotions are being used (Carlson et al., 2006). Adlerian therapists are less interested in what causes emotion than in how the emotions fit within the overall style of life. Let's look at some examples. Anger can be used to push people away or coerce others to submit. Apathy can be used to create power, because if people do not care about anything, it is difficult to control them. Shame is used to make one feel that there is something wrong with oneself; thus, it can create discouragement. Love is an emotion generated when people want to move toward something. Someone whose dominant motive is attachment to others will love people. Another person who has a dominant motive of security will love safety. Again, all emotions are in the service of the lifestyle of the person.

Lifestyle Types or Typologies

Adlerians have proposed several lifestyle types (Mosak & Di Pietro, 2006), the following are among the most common (Ansbacher & Ansbacher, 1956). It is important to note that no two people have the same exact lifestyle, nor do any of us fit completely into only one of the types.

- *Ruling.* This individual is dominant in relationships. There is a lot of initiative toward others, but little social interest in others. This is someone who has to be the boss.

- *Getting.* This individual expects things from others and is dependent on them. Little initiative and social interest are shown. They are happy as long as they get what they want.

- *Avoiding.* This individual shies away from problems. Similar to the previous lifestyles, there is minimal social interest or concern for others. They believe "nothing ventured, nothing lost" and attempt to avoid contact with others and their problems.

- *Driving.* This individual wants to achieve. Desperately. It is a matter of either "total success" or "total failure," with nothing in between. Achievement may result, but at the expense of others' interests.

- *Controlling.* Such individuals enjoy order, but it must be *their* order. A great deal of activity is expended toward keeping things predictable and avoiding surprises. Social interest is minimal because others in the system are constantly disrupting the individual's plans.

- *Victimized.* This person feels like life treats them unfairly or poorly.

- *Being good.* The individual satisfies a sense of superiority by being more competent, more useful, more right, and "holier than thou." Heightened activity and interest characterize this select club, to which very few can belong.

- *Being socially useful.* The individual cooperates with others and contributes to the social well-being without self-aggrandizement. Activity and social interest are both significant and constructively directed.

Assessing Lifestyle

Traditionally, lifestyle was assessed in a clinical setting through a structured and detailed interview schedule (Carlson et al., 2006). A formal lifestyle inventory is conducted following the guidelines outlined in Shulman and Mosak's (1988) *Manual for Life Style Assessment.* This formal process collects information on physical development, gender-guiding lines, sibling constellation, family atmosphere, early recollections, and so on. The end result is an accurate picture of an individual and their lifestyle. The drawback to this comprehensive collection of information is that it takes a minimum of eight to 10 sessions to complete, and Adlerians at times experience difficulties making comparisons across individuals and groups, limiting the ability for larger research about lifestyle (Gallagher, 1998). Adlerian therapists with time constraints might use a modified lifestyle inventory along the lines of the instrument that is based on the work of Roy Kern. We have included a version of this in the Appendix.

A lifestyle assessment will also include the collection of *early recollections* (ERs), which are the discrete, earliest memories that an individual can recall from under the age of 8 years. Adlerian therapists believe that people retain these memories as summaries of their current philosophy of life and therefore they can be used to help interpret current behavior (Clark, 2002, 2013; Mosak & Di Pietro, 2006). They are collected and used by the Adlerian therapist as a projective technique like a Rorschach inkblot test. According to Mosak and Di Pietro (2006), ERs have been the major assessment device for Adlerian therapists since Adler's original article on them. He indicated that they provide the life story or a glimpse at the lifestyle of each individual. Specifically, the clinician discovers how one will think, feel, and act as well as one's ethical convictions.

To standardize and simplify the collection of lifestyle information, the BASIS–A Inventory (Basic Adlerian Scales for Interpersonal Success—Adult Form Inventory) was created. The BASIS–A Inventory was developed from years of research on the concept of lifestyle and personality attributes and has been correlated with the MMPI, 16PF, Myers–Briggs, MCMI–II, SASSI–2, SCL–90–R, Bass Leadership Questionnaire, Dyadic Adjustment Scale, Beck Depression Inventory, and the Coping Resource Inventory for Stress (CRIS), among others (Curlette, Wheeler, & Kern, 1993). It continues to be used extensively in Adlerian-based research studies, with topics and populations of interest that include substance use, adjudicated youth and prison inmates, business leadership and management styles, counselor development and supervision, eating disorders, and many other mental health diagnoses. In addition to research, the BASIS–A Inventory is used in clinical mental health practice, supervision, and business and organization settings. For more information and/or to order, visit the website (http://www.basis-a.com).

There are five main scales and five supplemental scales. The five main scales are Belonging/Social Interest (BSI; measures how one finds belonging and contributes to one's community, either with large groups of people or more one-on-one), Going Along (GA; measures how much one values rules and expectations or engages in creative, independent thinking), Taking Charge (TC; measures how much one gravitates toward leadership opportunities or is more of a follower), Wanting Recognition (WR; measures how much one seeks outside approval from others or is more internally motivated), and Being Cautious (BC; measures how much one trusts others and views life as manageable/predictable or how much one takes a skeptical stance and sees people and life as unpredictable). The five supplemental scales are Harshness (H; corroborates the BC score as an indicator of how unpredictable childhood experiences were), Entitlement (E; measures how much one perceives he/she received special attention growing up), Liked By All (L; measures how much one desires to be liked by others), Striving for Perfection (P; measures how much one believes he/she can set goals and achieve them, akin to self-efficacy), and Softness (S; measures how much one is optimistic about life). The scales, like puzzle pieces, collectively provide Adlerian practitioners with a comprehensive understanding, or picture, of an individual's lifestyle and how that individual views self, others, and the world.

It is important to reinforce that cultural considerations are crucial in the assessment of the lifestyle, which may be determined based on connections with others in and outside the family (Frevert & Miranda, 1998). Therefore, the lifestyle assessment needs to be guided by the cultural beliefs and norms of clients in order to gain an accurate understanding of the clients within their environment. For example, for many Latinos, self-identity is related to a wide support network that includes family and friends. Perkins-Dock (2005) suggested that the Adlerian approach is effective for working with African Americans because it explores and accepts community and nonkinship relationships as part of the family constellation.

Basic Mistakes and Core Fears

Basic mistakes are the self-defeating attitudes and beliefs of an individual's lifestyle. Albert Ellis's rational emotive behavior therapy, Aaron Beck's cognitive therapy, and Arnold Lazarus's multimodal therapy all have their own terms that have built upon the notion of basic mistakes. All of these approaches share Adler's belief that people are not so much upset by things and other people as *they tend to upset themselves* by the ways they choose to think. Basic mistakes represent examples of cognitions that can be disputed and changed. Basic mistakes often reflect avoidance or withdrawal from others, excessive self-interest, or the desire for power. Mosak (2005) lists five of the more common basic mistakes.

1. *Overgeneralizations.* "There is no fairness in the world" or "Everyone hates me."
2. *False or impossible goals.* "I must please everyone if I am to be loved" or "Only when I am perfect will people love me."
3. *Misperceptions of life and life's demands.* "Life is so very difficult for me" or "Nobody can enjoy life in Chicago because it is so windy."
4. *Denial of one's basic worth.* "I'm basically stupid, so why would anyone want anything to do with me?"
5. *Faulty values.* "I must get to the top, regardless of who gets hurt in the process."

One additional area in which Adlerian theory has been especially helpful is identifying and addressing *core fears.* An Adlerian lens can be used to examine the most common fears presented by clients. Those that have been identified usually include the following areas (Dinkmeyer & Sperry, 2000; Shulman, 1973):

- *Fear of being imperfect.* It is one of our deepest, darkest secrets that each of us is a fraud. Adlerian therapists help their clients to become aware of this fear of phoniness and develop the "courage to be imperfect."
- *Fear of being vulnerable.* The more we authentically and honestly reveal our thoughts, the more likely it becomes that others will discover what we do not know. We spend our lives pretending to know and understand far more than we really do. With complete genuineness, we gain intimacy, but with intimacy comes vulnerability and we risk rejection. Adlerian therapists create safe settings where clients can honestly share how they think and feel. Clients can learn to be authentic and honest without the fear of being rejected.

- *Fear of disapproval.* Everyone wants to be loved and appreciated almost all the time. Though that might not be possible, it appears to be an eternal search. The more people risk connecting with others and showing their true selves, the more they are at risk for being hurt. Adlerian therapists help clients realize that it is impossible to please everyone and there are many who may not want to be loved or appreciated by us.
- *Fear of responsibility.* We all make mistakes in life, some of which we regret. It is easy to think, "If I only could have done things differently. If I only could start over." Adlerian therapists help their clients to choose to move on and stop suffering from past regrets.

Basic Life Tasks

Adlerian therapists believe that the questions and challenges of life can be grouped into five major *life tasks.* Adler identified the first three as coping with (a) the problems of social relationships, (b) the problems of work, and (c) the problems of love. Think about it this way: What are the issues that individuals and couples generally fight about and bring to therapy for resolution? Most often they are disputes over children, money, and sex, which are variations of the themes that Adler originally identified. Later, other important life tasks were added: (d) coping with self (Dreikurs & Mosak, 1967) and understanding existence (Mosak, 2005) represented "existential" dimensions that made the Adlerian theory more robust because it opened space for looking at one's own issues, as well as their meaning within a larger, social context. Finally, tasks associated with (e) parenting and the family (Dinkmeyer, Dinkmeyer, & Sperry, 1987) were added to address the task of coping with family concerns. Even after all these decades since these ideas were developed, there are still precious few frameworks that embrace so many valuable ideas. To be healthy according to an Adlerian means to have mastered all of the basic life tasks. Struggles occur with failures in any of the areas. When clients come to therapy, it is often due to difficulties with one or more of the basic life tasks. Another common goal of therapy becomes helping clients modify their lifestyles to more successfully navigate a task.

It is important to note that the tasks of life also reveal the relational aspect of Adlerian psychology. Watts (2012) noted that the five tasks address intimate, loving relationships; relationships with friends and others in society; relationships at work; one's relationships with oneself; and one's relationship with a Higher Power or the universe itself.

Social Interest

Adlerian therapists believe that every individual has a responsibility to the community, as well as to oneself. *Social interest* is a layered Adlerian term that is used to measure people's concern for other people (Bass, Curlette, Kern, & McWilliams, 2002). It is the altruistic drive or the basic need to give to others that all people possess. Social interest is an inadequate translation of *Gemeinschaftsgefühl*, the German word used by Adler. The word is more meaningfully translated when broken down into its parts. *Gemein* is "a community of equals," *shafts* means "to create or maintain," and *Gefühl* is "social feeling." Taken together, *Gemeinschaftsgefühl* means a community of equals creating and maintaining social feelings and interests; that is, people working together as equals to better themselves as individuals and as a community. Roughly defined, social interest is the kind of empathic bonding people feel for each other and the responsible actions and attitudes they take toward one another, a sense of belonging and participating with others for the common good. It takes into account that we all are members of the human community; we all have a responsibility to create a better world (Ansbacher, 1992b). Ansbacher noted that "community feeling" is the closest translation of the term, embracing a broad sense of affinity between people that, Adler clarified, can also extend to animals, the environment, and the cosmos.

According to Kurt Adler (1994), the tragedy of World War I had a deep impact on his father and the numerous shell-shocked soldiers and victims he treated. These experiences led Alfred Adler to the conclusion that civilization needed more social feeling rather than individualism. Adler was convinced that most of the people lacked adequate social feeling due to childhood feelings of inferiority (sometimes producing an inferiority complex or a compensatory and paradoxical superiority complex). To address this, Adler began to espouse the importance of social or community feeling. He believed that emotionally healthy people possessed social feeling in strong measure and could encourage it in others (King & Shelley, 2008).

Adler's biographer Phyllis Bottome (1939) noted that social interest was essentially "love thy neighbor" and was the same as the goal of all true religions. Adler, not a religious man, was prepared to do what no man of science had as yet accomplished—harness his science to a religious goal—in order to train human beings in such a way that the goal could actually be reached.

Social interest is a way to describe how community feeling can be expressed through behavior and can guide people to act in a socially useful manner (Ansbacher, 1992b). Rather than wanting to be or being "social," social interest is a sense of belonging and participating with others for the common good. It includes the notion of striving to make the world a better place. As social interest develops and increases, feelings of inferiority decrease. Social interest can be expressed on affective, cognitive, and behavioral levels (Stein & Edwards, 1998), and it can be expressed and experienced via connection online and in virtual environments (Hammond, 2015).

Social interest has also been connected to the experience and expression of empathy (Clark, 2007; Watts, 1998). Adler (1979) offered an understanding of social interest that resonates with empathy and understanding: "To see with the eyes of another, to hear with the ears of another, to feel with the heart of another" (p. 42). It appears clear from Adler's own words that empathy is included in the overall experience of social interest. Ansbacher (1983) noted that social interest "means not merely an interest in others but an interest in the interests of others" (p. 85). Individuals with developed social interest are able to "understand and appreciate [clients'] subjective experiences, their private worlds, and their opinions. Such an individual is tolerant, that is, he is reasonable, understanding, able to empathize, to identify with" (Ansbacher, 1992b, p. 36).

Adlerian therapists consider social interest so important that they often use it as a measure of mental health (Carlson et al., 2006), noting that the inability to belong or to connect with others results in pathology (Shifron,

2010). Mosak (1989) stated that persons with social interest are "socially contributive people interested in the common welfare and, by Adler's pragmatic definition of normality, mentally healthy" (p. 67). Murderers and others with antisocial personalities would, of course, be seen as having low social interest, as would anyone who is unduly selfish. Adler believed that therapy could play an important role to help clients not only resolve their individual difficulties but also develop greater concern and compassion for others. Paradoxically, developing greater compassion for others also helps clients resolve their individual problems. Adlerians routinely suggest that, as part of the treatment plan, their clients complete acts of kindness and generosity to others. This shifts the focus off of the self and onto others after teaching clients that it is through giving that we receive.

Social interest affects the lifestyle. When we have social interest, we find our place in life in a fashion that is good for all. It is a lifestyle in which the individual thinks of others and not just the self (Carlson et al., 2006). Mosak (2005) suggested that social interest could be viewed as evolving in three stages. The first stage is *aptitude*, which is the notion that everyone is born with the potential for cooperation and social living, but at this early stage, one's capacity to feel successful and connected to others is strongly shaped by the parent–child bond and relationships within one's family constellation. At the second stage, *ability*, the aptitude for social interest has developed and the person begins to express social interest through social cooperation in various activities. The last stage is referred to as *secondary-dynamic characteristics*, which builds upon the ability to integrate social interest into multiple aspects of one's lifestyle.

Social interest is at the root of all major religions and is the way of life in many non-Western countries (Alizadeh, 2012; Erickson, 1984; Watts, 2000a). For example, community or other focus is at the heart of living in most Latin and Asian countries (Carlson, Englar-Carlson, & Emavardhana, 2011, 2012). Alizadeh (2012), in noting the parallels between Islam and social interest, observed, "Within Islam, people are not alone, and God is with them and inside their hearts. This heart should be kept healthy (*ghalb-e salim*), and the best way to maintain that health is to live with people, with an equal regard for them" (p. 222).

Social interest may also be influenced by cultural identity. The Adlerian concepts of an interest in helping others, contributing to the social community, and social belonging support the cultural value system of many African American families (Boyd-Franklin, 1989; Parham, 2002; Perkins-Dock, 2005). The African-centered worldview is based in the notion that all things are connected, which helps to account for the connection between African American people and the sociocultural contexts in which they live (Parham, 2002). This sense of connection and commonality is consistent with the Adlerian construct of social interest (Perkins-Dock, 2005). Miranda et al. (1998) studied the mental health of Latinos by looking at the social-interest levels of three groups of Latinos: those who were highly acculturated to mainstream U.S. culture, those who were not acculturated, and those who were strongly bicultural and retained connection to beliefs and practices of the native and the host culture. They found that bicultural Latinos had higher levels of social interest than both the Latinos low in acculturation and those high in acculturation. They posited that bicultural Latinos had higher levels of adjustment and were more self-efficacious during the acculturation process due to connections with the host and native communities. The Thai practice of *metta* is another concept that is parallel with developing social interest (Carlson et al., 2011, 2012). Metta involves sending blessings of peace, happiness, freedom, and safety to those you love, those who are neutral, and those who are upsetting to you. This allows for the development of compassion and harmony with other people. The notion of *making metta* each day corresponds to a daily affirmation in connecting with one's local community toward the goal of promoting good. Carlson (2015b) suggested that metta or loving-kindness meditation could be called "Adlerian meditation" since the concepts are so similar.

Compensation for Inferiority and Superiority

Adler theorized that the central human directionality is toward competence or self-mastery; therefore, people strive for superiority (Watts, 2012). This does not mean that people try to be better than or over others, but that there is a human desire to naturally try and move from a perceived-weakened position to a perceived-positive one. In particular, that striving is for "both oneself and the common good of humanity" (Watts, 2012, p. 43). In fact, selfish striving solely for personal gain would be viewed as maladjustment, whereas healthy development follows the goal of community feeling and social interest. Adler (Ansbacher & Ansbacher, 1956) noticed that people often compensated for weaknesses, physical inferiorities, or perceived inadequacies in many ways. Painters and artists often have visual problems. Professional speakers, actors, and singers often stutter or have speech impediments, while musicians often have hearing difficulties. Adler did not believe in cause-and-effect theory, and he held that individuals have the creativity to turn weakness into strength. He noticed that rather than destroying people, problems have the potential to serve as catalysts and motivate individuals to turn perceived deficits into strengths. This is akin to Nietzsche's (1888) famous statement on adversity, "What doesn't kill us makes us stronger."

Even the most confident of people experience feelings of inferiority some of the time. In fact, feeling insignificant and disempowered is normal and universal (Watts, 2012). Inferiority feelings are global, subjective, and evaluative; generalizations that tend to be held onto despite evidence to the contrary. For example, if you are a student of psychotherapy theory, it is likely that you are feeling inferior in your developing understanding and skills as a practitioner. Clients themselves can be perplexing, and it is not uncommon to feel unsure of how to help. The good news, though, is that feelings of inferiority can serve as catalysts, motivating people to strive harder to reach their goals—and to learn more about psychotherapy in order to be a better, more helpful practitioner.

An *inferiority complex*—feelings of inferiority in large doses—can cause an individual to feel discouraged, dispirited, and incapable of proactive development. Basically, they give up. However, when one has inferiority feelings, one often compensates and strives for superiority. We see this often in the sports and entertainment worlds. For example, the Olympic track star Wilma Rudolph had polio as a child and was never supposed to walk, let alone become the world's fastest woman. The Olympic gold medalist and Major League baseball player Jim Abbott was born with only one arm. He compensated and became a dominant pitcher. Bethany Hamilton had her arm bitten off by a shark at the age of 13, yet she recovered to become a professional surfer.

Goals and Belonging

A central tenet of Adlerian theory is that all behavior is goal directed. People are constantly striving to reach self-declared goals that they believe will lead to happiness and satisfaction. All people are trying to find their place in the social world. During this process, they may engage in behavior that appears to be unhelpful to them and is often disruptive to others. Yet it is important to remember that all behavior makes sense to the behaver. There are many types of goals—conscious, nonconscious, short-term, long-term—but Adler believed that the ultimate goal of all people is to strive for significance and belonging. Ideally, goals are also a way of moving toward social interest. Adlerian therapists, for example, believe that children misbehave for one of four possible goals: (a) attention, (b) power, (c) revenge, or (d) inadequacy. Of course, like any summary, this list is simplistic, as motives are often much more complex and interwoven.

- A child with a goal of *attention* believes: "I only count when people notice me." Therefore they will behave in ways, positive and negative, that get them noticed by others.
- A child who has a goal of *power* believes: "I only count if I am powerful and have the last word." Therefore, they will behave in ways that challenge others, such as arguing or defiance.
- A child with a goal of *revenge* feels hurt and tries to hurt back in order to even the score. They think to themselves, and may articulate to others: "The only way I can protect myself is to do whatever I can to keep you at a distance and teach you there is a price to be paid for messing with me."
- A child with a goal of *inadequacy* feels worthless and wants others to view them as incapable: "I may not have much going for me," such a person might think, "but the good news is that it keeps people from expecting much from me and learning just how incapable I am."

Many professionals do not understand children's goal-directed motivation and try in vain to change children's behavior; in this way, they actually unknowingly strengthen the problem. Reminding, yelling, coaxing, and scolding often stop misbehavior for the short term because the child's goal of attention has been reached. Arguing with a child who has a goal of power seems to support the value of being powerful by modeling what you are hoping to stop. Hurting with excessive punishment makes the child with a goal of revenge feel more entitled to hurt back.

Family Constellation and Birth Order

One of Adler's important contributions to psychology was the recognition that birth order had an influence on the development of one's personality (Eckstein & Kaufman, 2012; Stewart, 2012). Whereas many theorists have discussed the importance of birth order, Adler was unique in recognizing that birth order occurs within the family constellation. Thus, understanding one's family system and how one interprets it was paramount to making sense of birth order and family dynamics (McKay, 2012). The *family constellation* is the term that was coined by Adler and developed by Dreikurs to signify the family or family system (Griffith & Powers, 2007). The term is similar to the one in astronomy that refers to a group of bodies in motion with each finding its place in relation to the other bodies. Dreikurs (1973) referred to it as the sociogram of the group at home during a child's formative years.

The way birth order affects the ways a person might develop is now taken for granted, but Adler (Ansbacher & Ansbacher, 1956) was among the first to observe that sibling position is a critical variable to consider, and he incorporated the concept of birth order into his work. Clearly, the eldest child does not grow up in the same psychological family, nor have the same parents, as the younger brothers and sisters. With their firstborn, parents are relatively insecure and unskilled. And for a while at least, the firstborn is the only child in the family. With younger siblings, the parents are more relaxed and knowledgeable, and, of course, younger siblings never experience being the only child. Adlerians have made considerable use of the concept in their clinical work. Before going any further, however, we need to point out an important distinction. Shulman and Mosak (1988) noted two definitions of birth order. *Ordinal position* refers to the actual order of birth of the siblings, whereas *psychological position* refers to the role the child adopts in his or her interactions with others. Adlerians are interested in the psychological position. Although the ordinal position will create a context, each person will interpret their place in the family differently. Individuals develop a style of relating to others in childhood and carry this into their adult interactions. Adlerians understand that the research studies that have discounted the value of birth order are only using ordinal position.

Adlerians discuss five psychological birth-order positions: only children, oldest born, second born, middle children, and youngest born. The characteristics that are listed below come from a review of over 200 empirical articles about birth-order research (Eckstein et al., 2010):

- *Only* children never have to share their world with siblings. They grow up using parents as models. Sometimes when children have significantly older (5 years or more) siblings, they are viewed more like only children rather than the youngest. Only children tend to be perfectionists with great needs for achievement who are used to having their way. They set their goals exceedingly high and tend to prefer polite distance from people. They are more likely to attend college, but also to have behavior problems.
- *Oldest* born are used to being first or number one. They are used to doing things independently. They are in charge and like being that way. Oldest born tend to be analytical, detailed, and methodical, and to overvalue control, sometimes expecting unrealistic perfection. It is for this reason that eldest children may have a tendency to try to do what is right. They tend to have the highest rate of academic success and are motivated high achievers. Oldest born are more likely to be leaders. By the time subsequent offspring arrive on the scene, parents have calmed down a bit. This results in the second, middle, or youngest children developing in ways that are different from their older siblings.

- *Second* born play the teeter-totter game with oldest born: where one goes up, the other goes down. If the oldest is good in math, the second will typically choose to ignore math and focus on areas that the oldest ignores, such as sports. Just as this occurs with academics, it occurs with personality traits. Second born tend to be rebellious, independent, and to dislike order. They are responders rather than initiators like their oldest-born siblings.
- *Middle* children are diplomats; they are people pleasers who dislike conflict but desire fairness and justice for all. They often feel squeezed by their siblings, and complain that they do not have the rights and privileges of oldest born nor the pampering and attention of youngest born. They are sociable by nature, but often have the greatest feelings of not fitting in. They tend to have the fewest acting-out problems and the highest rate of success in team sports.
- *Youngest* born are frequently excitement seekers who crave stimulation and are masters at putting others into their service. They are used to having things done for them, and they know how to play people's emotions quite well. Additionally, youngest born can often become the most ambitious in the family; feeling so far behind, they desire to "catch up" to the older ones to prove they are no longer the babies. They tend to have the highest social interest, be the most empathic, but are also the most rebellious and often overrepresented among clinical populations.

Birth order allows the Adlerian therapist to make some generalizations about individuals, but it is the individual that ultimately determines how they view their position in the family. Other factors that influence one's position include (Manaster & Corsini, 1982; Shulman & Mosak, 1977)

- *Age differences.* Closer together, the more competitive; further apart, the less influence.
- *Large families.* It is possible to have more than one "family."
- *Extrafamily competitors.* Families become complicated by remarriage, adoption, and their extended families.
- *Gender differences.* All boys or all girls, or having only one boy or girl can affect the family. Having transgender siblings could also apply here.

- *Death and survivorship.* Children are impacted by the death of a sibling.
- *Special siblings.* When one child is exceptional (e.g., athlete, scholar, mentally or physically challenged), everyone else is impacted.
- *Roles available.* Socioeconomic or cultural traditions may limit available roles.
- *Social views.* Physical appearance (e.g., skin color, body type) and level of overall attractiveness favors some and limits others.
- *Parental prejudice.* Parents have favorites.
- *Parents as models.* Parents intentionally or unintentionally guide their children through their own personalities and preferences.

Clearly, cultural considerations are important when looking at one's family constellation. Because the notion of family varies and the effects of gender and age also vary across cultures (McGoldrick, Giordano, & Garcia-Preto, 2005), Adlerian therapists take steps to define the family constellation based on one's concept of family and community. For example, if the first two children are girls and the next two are boys, it is possible that all of the sibling positions might be present. However, it is also possible that there could be an oldest boy and oldest girl as well as a youngest girl and youngest boy. In addition, the issue of filial piety can come into play and further influence the expression of birth order. Since parenting roles may be shared with grandparents and other adult relatives, fictive kin, and older siblings, it is important to look at how the client defines their family constellation. This is especially important in understanding modern-family types, such as blended, step, and chosen families.

Theory of Change

Adler firmly believed that change was both possible and desirable in all people. Therefore, Adlerian therapy is optimistic in that it stresses the potential of growth in each client. This confident worldview transmits hope and belief in the client, creating a type of self-fulfilling prophecy for clients. The Adlerian therapist believes that at any given time, each person is at a phase of growth and development. Whereas Adlerian therapists do emphasize the influence of biology and the importance of experience in early childhood, the Adlerian model has more of a "soft" determinism approach, "which is the notion that clients have conscious choices, probabilities, possibilities, and influences, not causes. Whereas Freud was interested in facts, Adler was interested in clients' beliefs about facts" (Sapp, 2006, p. 109). This notion suggests that clients are always in the process of becoming (Rogers, 1961).

Adlerian therapists do not follow the "medical model" orientation to maladjustment and instead embrace a nonpathological perspective (Sperry, Carlson, Sauerheber, & Sperry, 2015). Clients are not viewed as sick (as in having a disease) or mentally ill, and are not identified or "labeled" by diagnoses. Since Adlerian theory is grounded in the growth model of personality, clients are viewed as discouraged rather than sick. They are viewed as in need of a new outlook on life and a different skill set. Therefore, the process of change in Adlerian therapy is not about *curing* a client but about *encouraging and educating* a client. As previously mentioned, encouragement is considered a crucial facet of the process of change and a core aspect of growth and development (Mosak & Maniacci, 1999). For creating change, Adlerians know that encouragement works better than threats (Carlson et al., 2006). Encouragement skills include demonstrating concern for clients through active listening and empathy; communicating genuine respect for and confidence in clients; focusing on client strengths, assets, and resources; telling stories of how others have successfully coped with similar problems; helping clients generate alternatives for maladaptive beliefs; expressing confidence in the client's ability to change and pointing out the positive consequences of change; helping clients see humor in everyday experiences; and constantly focusing on effort and progress (Ansbacher & Ansbacher, 1956; Carlson & Slavik, 1997; Dinkmeyer & Losoncy, 1980; Main & Boughner, 2011; Watts, 2000b; Wong, 2015). The educational component may happen both within and outside of the psychotherapy session. Adlerian therapists use homework assignments that include reading, watching videos, directed behavioral assignments, and other ways to learn and develop the necessary life skills.

Adlerian therapists realize that all clients enter into treatment with different levels of readiness to change. They are aware of the different stages of change that their clients bring into treatment, such as those identified by Prochaska, Norcross, and DiClemente (2007): precontemplation, contemplation, determination, action, maintenance, and termination. The stages of change represent *when* people change, and the Adlerian therapist identifies the stage and tailors their treatment process (*how* people change) to match the stage (Norcross, Krebs, & Prochaska, 2011).

Once readiness to change is addressed, the next question becomes: What needs to be changed? Therapy is structured to help clients understand how they have a role or part in creating their problems and how they can take responsibility for their behavior. Further, it is structured to help them understand that often one's problems are related to faulty thinking and learning, but ultimately the client can assume responsibility for creating change (Mosak, 2005). When *mistaken goals* are revealed, clients can choose to pursue more appropriate goals with vigor and courage (Carlson et al., 2006). Mistaken goals include goals that are detrimental to others, such as those that run counter to social interest.

The change process in therapy begins with the creation of a positive therapist–client relationship. A good therapeutic relationship is a "friendly one between equals" (Mosak, 2005, p. 69). Adler believed that the client and therapist need to collaborate or create what is now referred to as a *treatment alliance* (Wampold, 2010) in order for change to take place. The Adlerian therapist understands the importance of goal alignment as a necessary component of this alliance. Dreikurs (1973) felt that once the client and therapist mutually agreed to work upon the same goal, the relationship has been cemented. To emphasize equality, Adler was the first therapist to come out from behind the couch and directly face the client.

Adlerian therapy methods break the process down into the following assumptions about how change occurs (Carlson et al., 2006):

1. Through therapy, a client can learn about mistaken goals. Once *aware* of these goals the client can decide either to change or not to change. Throughout this decision, the relationship between the therapist and client should be one of mutual respect.
2. By knowing mistaken goals, the client can recognize patterns in motivation and as a result develop insight. During this process, encouragement helps the client change behavior.

3. The Adlerian therapist also realizes that people do not just change from logic and insight but must be emotionally moved by gains they will make or pains they will be avoiding.
4. Because new behavior may work better in new situations than the old, the client may replace old private logic with a new common sense.
5. As the new common sense grows, the client may show more social interest. More social interest often results in a greater sense of belonging.
6. Feeling a sense of belonging can mean feeling equal to others, which has the effect of being even more encouraged. As this develops, the client feels more confident about their place in the world.
7. Because the client feels better about things, more risks may be taken because the client is less concerned about making mistakes. The client has gained the courage to be imperfect.

Therefore, in Adlerian therapy, change is a process that develops over time. Encouragement fills the client with hope, expectancy, and the courage to act. Throughout this process the client is gaining new insights and undertaking new behavior. Change is bound to follow. In Chapter 4, we highlight this process and the practice of Adlerian psychotherapy.

4

The Therapy Process

It is always easier to fight for one's principles than live up to them.

—Alfred Adler

In the previous chapter, we introduced a series of concepts that are central to the Adlerian approach to helping people. In this chapter, we address how to apply the concepts and ideas to the actual practice of Adlerian psychotherapy. We show the semistructured way an Adlerian therapist constructs the stages of therapy by following an actual case example in which the therapeutic stages and strategies are highlighted. We look at the therapist–client relationship and roles as well as some of the various Adlerian techniques and strategies before offering a second case example that highlights Adlerian theory in action.

Before moving into the therapy process, a caveat about Adlerian therapy is necessary. *Traditional,* or what is referred to as *classical* Adlerian

http://dx.doi.org/10.1037/0000014-004
Adlerian Psychotherapy, by J. Carlson and M. Englar-Carlson

psychotherapy, is a long-term treatment perhaps most similar to psychoanalysis. Henry Stein (2013) is one of the most prolific proponents of this approach, and it is also the form of Adlerian psychotherapy that is still practiced in many European countries. This book is not especially concerned with classical Adlerian psychotherapy; instead, it is focused on describing a more modern or contemporary individual, couple, and family therapy that pieces together Adlerian theory and techniques and is therefore short- or long-term depending on the needs of the client. Adler seemed to advocate training/education of the public before treatment (or therapy), noting that individuals and the community would profit more from primary prevention strategies (Ansbacher, 1992b) as a means to avert the need for psychotherapy altogether. So it appears that much of what people think of as Adlerian therapy is actually ways of teaching Adlerian concepts and principles about how to have a healthy life. The tools that Adler used, such as lifestyle analysis and open-forum family counseling, work well for this purpose but are not what we are specifically referring to in this book.

Even though a "contemporary" Adlerian model has been practiced, little has been written specifically about a complete modern Adlerian psychotherapy or talk therapy. Surprisingly, despite Adlerian psychotherapy being one of the oldest or original forms of treatment, it is also one of the least explored. "Brief" versions of Adlerian psychotherapy (Carlson, Watts, & Maniacci, 2006; Nicoll, Bitter, Christensen, & Hawes, 2000; Slavik, Sperry, & Carlson, 2000; Sperry, 1989; Wood, 2003) have been written about for several decades, but the contemporary model (between long analysis and brief therapy) has not been spelled out or featured before this volume.

ROLE OF THE THERAPIST–CLIENT RELATIONSHIP

It might be easy to deduce from the discussion in Chapter 3 how therapists using the Adlerian approach behave and what roles they take. Yet sometimes simplicity is deceiving, so let's review exactly what this looks like. The many adjectives that describe the Adlerian therapeutic relationship include cooperative, collaborative, egalitarian, optimistic, and respectful

(Bazzano, 2008; Watts, 1998, 2000b). Above all, the therapist is looking to create a growth-oriented alliance that emphasizes the client's strengths, abilities, and assets (Watts, 2000b).

An effective Adlerian therapist is one who can convey social interest to the client. In that sense, the therapist will try to model caring and empathy (Kottler, Englar-Carlson, & Carlson, 2013). Watts (1998) noted that Adler's connotation of therapist social interest looked very similar to Rogers's descriptions of person-centered therapy's core conditions of change (e.g., empathy, unconditional positive regard, congruence). Adler (1927b) thought that empathy with the client was critical to therapeutic success, observing, "It is essential for the practitioner to possess, in a considerable degree, the gift of putting himself in the other person's place" (p. 25). "The therapist has to put himself in the individual's place in order to see that for this particular individual a certain situation seems too difficult" (Adler, 1935, p. 9). The therapist needs to model empathy and caring for the client. Encouragement has been referred to as the therapeutic modeling of social interest (Carlson et al., 2006). Because of the Adlerian emphasis on social interest, it is also clear that social interest permeates and becomes a core aspect of the therapy relationship.

As noted in Chapter 3, the Adlerian therapist uses encouragement as a therapeutic tool—it permeates all interactions with the client. Encouragement is specifically important in supporting the client in the initial formation of the therapeutic alliance (Carlson et al., 2006). As many clients enter psychotherapy feeling discouraged, encouragement is critical in helping shape a client's perspective about the decision to be in therapy and the client's expectancy for a positive outcome. Positive expectancies in therapy (or hope) can produce better overall therapy outcomes (Constantino, Arnkoff, Glass, Ametrano, & Smith, 2011); thus, Adlerian therapy is sensitive to supporting a client's outcome expectations. Overall, Dreikurs (1967) thought that therapeutic success itself was largely dependent on the ability of the therapist to provide encouragement, and therapeutic failures were associated with the inability to encourage the client. In developing the therapeutic relationship, the therapist shows encouragement by demonstrating concerns for the client through active listening, conveying empathy, showing respect for clients, exhibiting confidence in the client's ability to create change, using hope-inspiring statements, focusing on client's assets and strengths, using humor to demonstrate perspective taking in life experiences, focusing on progress and effort, and working with clients to develop alternative positive-focused beliefs to replace discouraging ones (Carlson et al., 2006). Further, the therapist continually checks in on the client's outcome expectations and encourages accordingly, thus matching the client's stage of change.

Overall, the therapist is a positive participant in therapy and one who helps maintain hope and expectancy. The therapist is actively recruiting the client as a coparticipant and fellow worker in the therapy so that any successful outcome can be associated with the work and effort of the client (Overholser, 2010). This empowerment of the client is consistent with multicultural therapy approaches that value empowerment of clients to their own strengths (Hays, 2009). Already, it is clear that Adlerian therapists are a somewhat select bunch of individuals who are able to convey encouragement in their interpersonal relationships. Adler (1927c) thought that being a therapist demanded "a certain optimism and patience, and above all the exclusion of all personal vanity" (p. 11). The therapist believes in the client so the client can learn how to believe in him- or herself. The therapist is also personally humble, as a core therapist task is showing the client how to have the courage to be imperfect.

Adlerian therapy follows four stages, each of which builds on the previous stage. The first and most important stage is titled the *relationship*, as Adlerian therapy occurs in a relational context (Carlson et al., 2006; Watts, 2000b). The success of subsequent stages rests upon the further development and continuation of a good therapeutic relationship. In this relationship, the therapist creates a safe environment for clients to explore their mistaken beliefs, faulty values, and ineffective behavior. The subsequent stages (assessment, insight and interpretation, reorientation) all require the therapist to be an active participant in the therapy process. In many ways, due to the level of activity, constant encouragement, and the psychoeducational component, the therapist behaves very much like a coach who is helping someone develop a new life skill.

One aspect that might be a little different in Adlerian therapy is that at times, due to the psychoeducational component, the relationship might take on a teacher–student feel. This dynamic is present in the *assessment phase*, where the therapist educates the client about the assessment of the client's lifestyle and how effective this lifestyle is in reaching life goals. Adlerian therapists view education of alternative coping styles as a means of dealing with problems. They might also give their clients advice, yet the advice would be offered in more of a relationship of equals and in the spirit of helping another person out with their difficulties. Adlerian therapists do not decide for clients what their goals should be or what needs to change. This is determined collaboratively to allow clients to set and meet their own goals. Yet once goals are identified, Adlerian therapy becomes goal focused. Some of the methods for reaching the goals are determined by the therapist, yet the goals themselves rest with the client. The methods are also adapted to a client's cultural background. Interpretation and goal setting appear consistent with suggestions (Hays, 2009; Smith, Rodríguez, & Bernal, 2011) that effective multicultural therapy, specifically with Asian Americans (Smith et al., 2011; Sue & Zane, 1987), includes aspects of credibility (e.g., perception of the therapist as listening, empathic, effective, and trustworthy) and giving (e.g., client's perception that something was received from the therapeutic encounter) specific skills or easily articulated insights. Kim and Hogge (2013) described this process with a Korean woman diagnosed with *Hwa-byung*, a well-defended Korean anger syndrome. Adlerian concepts and principles (e.g., family constellation, lifestyle assessment in the cultural context, inferiority feelings, mistaken beliefs, exogenous factors, life tasks) were effective in conceptualizing and treating this problem in the cultural context.

CASE EXAMPLE WITH TECHNIQUES HIGHLIGHTED

To provide more insight into the process of Adlerian psychology, a detailed case example is presented. This case looks at the conceptualization of a client and the many ways in which an Adlerian might intervene. What follows is an introduction to the client. Then, throughout the chapter, we use examples and dialogue from this case to highlight different therapeutic interventions.

Antonio Gonzales came to therapy at the request of his wife, Rosa. A third-generation Latino male of Mexican heritage in his early 30s, Antonio had been very unhappy for several months. He willingly completed several assessment inventories that provided background information on his family-of-origin, lifestyle, and level of happiness. By his own report, Antonio came from a "dysfunctional" family. His parents never divorced, but they did not live together, nor did they raise their children. Antonio was actually raised by his grandfather, while his twin brother was raised by their grandmother. The grandparents lived in the same city, but they maintained separate homes, so the brothers grew up attending different schools and seldom saw each other.

Antonio's working-class urban neighborhood was "not an easy place to grow up." He managed to avoid legal problems, but he was frequently involved in fights, vandalism, and petty crime. Antonio's grandfather was a strong figure during his childhood and made sure that Antonio went to school, completed his schoolwork, and graduated from high school. Antonio had no explanation for his luck, but in spite of pretty average grades he was accepted to a small private college and was provided with financial aid. An average student, well liked by his professors and peers, Antonio managed to graduate in 4 years with an accounting degree. He had become an accounting major because he felt it would lead to a steady job, but he really would have preferred a career in social work. Antonio appreciated all that his grandfather did for him. He worked hard and managed to provide for all of Antonio's needs. He and Antonio attended the local parish Catholic Church and were active in the neighborhood social club. His grandfather had died 5 years ago, just after Antonio and Rosa were married. This loss was significant for Antonio, and he felt as though he no longer had a family. He resented his grandmother and parents for abandoning him and at the time had nothing to do with them or his brother.

Antonio's wife, Rosa, is Latina, is also of Mexican heritage, and is very close to her family. Her family lives far away, so she only sees them once or twice a year, although they talk daily on the phone. Rosa has one younger sister, who is currently in college and is also close to the family. Antonio likes Rosa's family, but he has a hard time getting close to them. He finds them a bit boring and dull, although they are successful and very religious. Though the family is welcoming to Antonio, he feels like they are "better" than him and thinks that they can't believe that Rosa ever agreed to marry him.

Both Rosa and Antonio work for the same large international accounting firm located near a large Midwestern city. They have both been employed there for 8 years. Rosa is a "star" and is being promoted at a quick rate. Antonio's career has been less successful, and he believes that he can't advance because of racial discrimination. Rosa believes this is just an excuse because she is also Mexican and is not being limited by race. While it was unknown whether Antonio was actually experiencing some racial discrimination, the differing view between Antonio and Rosa was causing friction in their marriage and affecting their ability to talk about their work life. Further, with Rosa's most recent promotion, her salary is now nearly twice that of Antonio. The couple has one son, Jorge, who attends child care at the firm. Jorge is a happy 2-year-old and the pride of both parents. They are planning to have more children and have discussed the possibility of Antonio's becoming a full-time stay-at-home parent and taking care of their children and the household.

Antonio presented for psychotherapy because over the past few months he has felt angry, down, and by his admission, "discombobulated." He hated his job and the "poor treatment" he had been receiving. While his job was a drag, Antonio taught the adolescent religion class at their local Catholic parish and seemed to really enjoy working with the youth. He mentioned that being with Jorge and teaching were the two things he looks forward to the most. Antonio said that he would like to quit his job and go back to school to become a social worker. Rosa was supportive of this goal and told Antonio to do this, but he didn't seem to be willing to make any changes and take the steps to see what this career shift might entail.

As part of the early assessment, Antonio was asked to recount some early recollections. These early recollections are viewed as one of the most direct ways to assess and understand the lifestyle, as early recollections often help clarify goals and strivings for significance (Clark, 2002). Antonio provided the following early recollections:

- *Early recollection 1.* "I was 4 years old and I remember there was an ice cream truck going by my house. I really wanted ice cream, but just stood and watched it. I remember the bells ringing and the pictures of kids eating ice cream on the side of the truck. The most vivid part was feeling empty as the truck passed me by."
- *Early recollection 2.* "I must have been in first grade so I was 6 or so. The teacher was picking kids to be the captains for our recess kickball game. I was the best player, so I was sure she would select me as a captain. She never even looked my way as she picked Paul and Ferd instead. The most vivid part was my sad feeling and thinking that I would not get to play, but I am sure I did get to play. It just hurt."
- *Early recollection 3.* "I was 6 or so and we were playing on the playground. Somebody kicked the ball to me and I caught it. When I kicked it back, a little kid ran in front of me and the ball hit him so hard he was knocked down and started to cry. I said I was sorry but no one believed me. The most vivid part was seeing the look on the other kid's face when I was trying to explain that I did not mean it. I felt hurt and all alone."

As part of the early recollection assessment process, clients are asked to reflect on the meaning of the early recollections and to comment on any patterns. This process helps build rapport while engaging the client in the collaborative counseling process as an involved partner.

Therapist: Do you see any pattern or similarity among the three recollections?

Antonio: They seem to be situations where things didn't work out very well for me.

Therapist: Could it be that "no matter what I do things never work out the way I want them to"? The goodies in life pass you by, you are the best player but not picked, and no one believes your story.

Antonio: (His eyes fill with tears.) Nothing seems to work for me.

Therapist: I am confused. I thought you had a beautiful and successful wife. A healthy and handsome son. Good health and an okay job. Even your in-laws like you!

Antonio: But not the important things. Why can't I be successful at my job? Why don't I have more friends? Why can't I do what I like doing? I don't even have a family.

Therapist: Although many important things are going well, there still are some big hurts and voids that need to be addressed that have you upset and feeling unfulfilled.

Antonio: Where do you think would be a good place to start? I mean, you are right, there are so many good things in my life yet I am still not happy.

Antonio needed some encouragement to make the changes in his life that could increase his happiness. Although he appeared happy to be in therapy and wanted his life to be better, Antonio was stuck in his life and in his way of doing things. Although he felt like a total failure, a review of his life showed that he was only a failure in some areas, and this was reflected back to him. The therapist used positive empathy (Conoley, Pontrelli, Oromendia, Carmen Bello, & Nagata, 2015) to tap into Antonio's desire for a new job and direction in life that provided more satisfaction. This positive responding by the therapist helped Antonio to realize the therapist was possibly different from those that saw him in a negative light and maybe more like his grandfather. His grandfather was always supportive of the growth aspects of Antonio's life and situation, and this therapist was similar. The therapist was hopeful that this reframing helped Antonio to see his problem from a different perspective—that when these feelings occur he shuts down and lets opportunity pass him by. He realized that this was happening at work. When things didn't go the way he hoped, he would "cop an attitude and piss off everyone in the office."

An early session with Antonio was devoted to teaching him some anger management and mindfulness meditation skills for awareness, self-calming, and self-compassion. A discussion ensued about Antonio's anger and whether he saw any connections to his past or his identity as a Mexican American man. Antonio reflected that his adolescence had been difficult and that in many ways among his peers he outwardly displayed the stereotypical aggression and chauvinism of *machismo* (Arciniega, Anderson, Tovar-Blank, & Tracey, 2008). At the same time, Antonio spoke fondly of his grandfather and how he showed him something else, which was *caballerismo* (Glass & Owen, 2010), the positive side of machismo, which includes dignity, honor, respect, familial responsibility, and a father's role as a provider (Arciniega et al., 2008; Falicov, 2010). With some emotion in his eyes, Antonio commented that his anger at work was his machismo rising up and that he hated that part of himself but that he desired to be more of a man and father like his grandfather, so that he could be that person for little Jorge. The therapist proposed that maybe his anger at work was coming from a good place, namely, the desire to be a better provider working in a job that offered Antonio some dignity, honor, respect for the work, and also for himself. Antonio liked the notion that he was striving to become more of a *caballero* since it helped him understand himself from a more positive, prosocial perspective. Antonio expressed a desire "to do something," and the therapist responded by offering some specific skills.

Antonio: I am just so tense all the time. I get angry at the drop of a hat. Rosa says that I need to learn to "chill" and learn to be calmer . . . especially at work.

Therapist: What have you tried so far to calm down?

Antonio: I try not to react but that never helps. I thought about taking a yoga class, but I don't have the time.

Therapist: Many people have found that mindfulness meditation can help to reduce both anxiety and anger. It has something to do with the frontal lobe of the brain. Is that something that might interest you?

Antonio: I would rather do that than take pills like the doctor suggested.

Therapist: Would you be able to free up the first 10 or 15 minutes of the day?

Antonio: Sure. Rosa usually gets up with Jorge in the morning.

Therapist: Find a quiet place where you can sit with your back straight in a chair. Begin to focus on your breathing. Breathe in slowly and deeply. As you inhale, say, "I am," and when you exhale, say the word *calm*. Say it in your mind and not out loud. When you find that your mind has wandered off to other thoughts just let them go and come back to "I am . . . calm."

This was a beginning meditation for Antonio, and other interventions follow below.

THERAPY STAGES

Adlerian therapy proceeds along a series of progressive stages that seem quite logical. In practice the stages are not necessarily followed in a fixed, sequential fashion but are actually fluid, stopping and starting many times as therapy progresses. The four stages of Adlerian therapy are as follows.

Stage I: The Relationship

The first step in any therapeutic encounter is to establish a *collaborative* relationship. This is an empathic, supportive relationship, one that is based on democratic principles and essential equality. The Adlerian therapist uses all the standard skills favored by any other professional at this stage, using well-timed questions and reflections of feeling and content, in order to build a solid alliance. Empathy and support are used to establish a sense of trust and what is referred to as the *treatment alliance*. Adlerians believe that once the therapist and client have collaborated and mutually agreed on the goals of therapy, this alliance is established. If that doesn't happen first, subsequent therapeutic efforts are likely to be less than successful.

Stage II: Assessment

In the next stage, the therapist conducts a comprehensive assessment of the client's functioning. Assessing the lifestyle and the goals behind it is critical in Adlerian psychotherapy (Peluso, 2012). This occurs through a

combination of inventories like the lifestyle scale, reviewing early recollections, and a clinical interview. The therapist gathers information about
how the client is seeking to belong in the social world of family, school,
work, friends, and marriage (committed relationships). The basic beliefs
are often uncovered through information on the family constellation and
the client's early recollections. Their beliefs will also be reflected through
a person's current convictions, attitudes, and priorities.

In the Appendix, we include a *lifestyle assessment* to highlight the areas
that Adlerian therapists would explore in depth. A structured format like this
is used by many therapists of all persuasions and backgrounds, regardless
of whether they affiliate as Adlerian or not. In this assessment, a thorough
history is explored, including family background, belief systems, cultural
heritage, educational level, personal goals, and other facets of being human.
As you would expect, early recollections are also collected. The therapist
asks the client, "I would like to hear about some early memories. Think
back to a time when you were very young, under the age of 8, as early as
you can remember, and tell me something that happened one time. Be
sure to recall something you clearly remember, not something you were
told about by others." There are three guidelines to collecting early recollections. First, the early recollection or memory must be a single, one-
time event that has a narrative. Second, it must be visualized. Third, two
parts must be clearly articulated: (a) the most vivid part of the recollection and (b) how the client felt during the recollection. Generally, eight
to 10 early recollections are gathered, but the pattern is often clear with
as few as three.

Other questions asked during the assessment phase can include

- *Family constellation.* "What was it like for you growing up?" "What roles
  did you play in your family?"
- *Social relationships.* "To whom are you closest?" "What is most satisfying to you about your friendships?"
- *Work life.* "How do you feel about your job?"
- *Sexuality.* "What are the most and least satisfying aspects of your sexual
  relationship with your partner?"

- *Sense of self.* "How do you feel about who you are and the ways you have developed?"
- *Sense of identity.* "Who are three people I should know if I am to really understand who you are?"

In addition to these specific Adlerian-based inquiries, clients would be asked other questions in the exploration phase of the relationship.

- "What would you like help with?"
- "What are you expecting or hoping that therapy might do for you?"
- "How would you like things to be different after our sessions are over?"
- "What have you already tried in your efforts to take care of your concerns?"
- "What support is available to you during this difficult time?"
- "What are things that YOU will need to personally change in order to feel better?"
- "What are some of the strengths and assets you bring to our relationship?"

These are the sorts of questions an Adlerian therapist would bring up in a session with a new client. These questions can be viewed as Socratic, as the purpose is to engage the client in a dialogue to help uncover the assumptions and evidence that underpin their thoughts in respect to their concerns (Carey & Mullan, 2004). Careful use of questioning enables the therapist to challenge recurring or isolated instances of a client's thinking and basic mistakes while maintaining an open position that respects the client's internal logic to even the most seemingly illogical thoughts (Stein, 1991). They help the therapist to efficiently and quickly gather background information, assess preliminary expectations, and find out what the client has already done or attempted.

During the assessment stage, the focus is on the person in their social and cultural context (Debb & Blitz, 2010). Adlerian therapists look for clients to define themselves within their social environments; they do not try and fit clients into a preconceived model. Adlerian therapists explore salient cultural-identity aspects such as age, race, ethnicity, lifestyle, and gender to emerge in therapy and then attend to a client's individual meaning of their own culture identity and worldview (Sperry, 2015). They emphasize the value of subjectively understanding the unique cultural world of the individual. For clients from racial or ethnic minorities, this allows therapists to assess the importance of a macro view of the client's ethnicity within the micro view of the client's individuality. This provides the opportunity to assess acculturation and racial identity within the client's lifestyle. This can also assist the therapist and the client to apply a culturally embedded understanding of what is considered "positive" or a "strength" (Pedrotti, 2011; Pedrotti, Edwards, & Lopez, 2009).

Stage III: Insight and Interpretation

In the third stage, the Adlerian therapist interprets the findings of the assessment in order to promote insight for the client. A therapist might say something such as, "It seems like life is unfair and you believe that you can't do anything to change this situation." This, of course, is not just a simple reflection of feeling and content, but rather an interpretation or confrontation of sorts, in that the client must examine the validity of this belief. Is it really true and accurate that a person is absolutely powerless, even if the world does sometimes *appear* to be unfair? The therapist takes an active role in the assessment and interpretation, and works with the client to see how the results help them make sense of their lifestyle and how they pursue their life goals. Adlerians will pay particular attention to basic mistakes in the lifestyle and in exploring how these contribute to a client's presenting concern, and then how a client can make changes in their approach to life to be more successful.

The therapist assists clients to develop a new orientation to life, one that is more fully functioning. For example, although you might believe that you can't do anything about a particular problem in your life right now, you have been successful with other challenges you have faced, many that seem to have been far more difficult than this. A client may be challenged along this same line: "You say that you are powerless with your husband, but I have noticed that you regularly stand up to your parents, your boss, and your children. I wonder what the difference is for you?" The therapist may find out what the client believes the client has done wrong in life.

For example, a young woman began therapy believing that if she were more perfect in appearance and behavior, then others would love her even more. She worked very hard at doing everything she possibly could to appear fashionable and well-groomed; she had a whole library of etiquette books to guide her behavior. Although this may seem like a reasonable self-development plan, it actually made her rather difficult for others to be around. She didn't seem to understand that one of the things that makes people attractive to others is not their perfection, but their imperfections. Real people make mistakes and have problems. They also have the courage to face their problems. She needed to understand how her strategy for creating perfection and closeness was actually creating distance and contempt from others.

A key approach to Adlerian therapy, as it is for other cognitive therapies, is to identify the thought disturbances and core fears that get in the way of being satisfied. In the third stage of therapy, Adlerian therapists are inclined to explore with clients their self-defeating thinking patterns that contribute to distorted perceptions (Carlson et al., 2006; Mosak & Maniacci, 1999).

Stage IV: Reorientation

Once clients develop sufficient insight into their problems, the therapy shifts to action. Insight can be a wonderful thing, but only if it leads to constructive movement toward desired goals. Smith et al. (2011) suggested that therapeutic methods for problem resolution that are consistent with the client's culture will be more compatible for the client. In that sense, an Adlerian therapist works with the client to create interventions that are culturally and personally congruent. For example, in Antonio's marriage, Rosa was very close to her family of origin, which might lead some therapists to see her as enmeshed with her family. Yet given her family's Mexican heritage and how closeness was expressed within the family in a loving rather than an emotionally smothering or limiting manner (Falicov, 2014), the therapist made a different assessment. The Adlerian therapist understands that family closeness is important to Rosa and is a given in her marriage to Antonio. Rather than suggesting that she become less involved with her family of origin, it is more important that she focuses on increasing her positive involvement with Antonio.

Because the Adlerian approach is both insight- and action-oriented, the therapist would not be shy in helping clients to convert their self-declared goals into specific homework assignments or tasks that can be completed between sessions. Adlerian therapists will give specific assignments that involve thinking, feeling, and responding in a different fashion. If a couple was not taking responsibility for their marriage, by taking it for granted and not spending quality time together, the therapist might suggest that they plan a "date" with their spouse. The therapist might also suggest that the clients do outside reading (i.e., bibliotherapy; see Carlson & Dinkmeyer, 2003) to learn about ways to strengthen their relationship and complete weekly homework-type structured activities to work on their relationship.

Throughout every step in the process, a collaborative, supportive relationship is used as leverage to keep the client motivated and to make progress. In *reorientation*, or moving from insight to action, the client is helped to make new choices that are more consistent with desired or stated goals.

For Antonio, one of the things he learned in therapy was that he wanted a career shift. Before therapy, he was aware of these thoughts but was not able or ready to accept them and attempt guided action toward a new career. At the reorientation stage, however, he was ready for movement or change.

Therapist: You say you don't really like accounting and would rather be out in the world helping others.

Antonio: I know I say that. I really like helping others, but there is no money in that work. I think I can help others through volunteer work.

Therapist: What things have you been thinking about doing?

Antonio: There are lots of things that I can do at church. They also seem to always be looking for coaches at the YMCA.

Therapist: So you think that would allow you to feel better by helping others? So what about your job?

Antonio: I don't mind accounting as long as I could be my own boss and make some more money.

Therapist: Antonio, it seems like over the past few months we have talked so much about how unhappy you are as an accountant and how it does not seem to really make you happy. And now here you are again settling for accounting. I doubt that freedom and more money will really fit your own goals.

Antonio: Hmm . . . yeah. Funny how easy it is for me to not let myself think about larger dreams or what I really want. So yes, there are so many things going well but my job is a constant drag that gets me stuck. Rosa tells me this, you tell me this, and I guess that deep down I tell myself the same thing— I need to do something else that makes me happier, and I do not think there is a happy future for me in accounting. I am ready for a new career.

Therapist: Can you think of a way to make that happen?

Antonio: I suppose I need to go to school, or talk to someone to help me out. As we have talked about before, I know that helping others is what makes me happy and motivated. Most of my life I have just done the minimum since the goals did not matter to me all that much. But I love being a dad, and I love working with the kids at the church, and I think I need to do something in social work or human services. And that means going back to school for a master's degree.

Therapist: Antonio, that is the first time I have heard you say that with such conviction—I actually believe you want this and that you are ready.

Antonio: It is funny you mention that because I am not sure I have said it before and actually thought that I would do it myself. But even just saying that to you makes me feel a bit better.

Therapist: Okay, so what is the next step, and what do you want to have happen?

The first step in the reorientation stage is to clearly identify what it is that the client wants most. These goals must be realistic and reasonable. A client might say that she wants to have more love in her life.

The therapist's next task would be to help her pinpoint just what it would mean for her to have more love. For one person, it might mean more friends; for another, more dates or perhaps a deeper relationship with a current partner. Through this process the therapist can help the client develop goals that are achievable. Almost any problem-solving method that the client and therapist come up with might be used to create a plan of action. That point is important to highlight because Adlerians are technically eclectic in the interventions they use.

It is at this point in the therapy process that the Adlerian practitioner may appear more like a coach or a teacher. The goal is to help clients to acquire the necessary skills and behaviors to create new patterns in their lives. These behaviors must also be consistent with their lifestyles, as defined earlier.

Let's look further at an example of this process in action. A woman came to therapy with the stated goal of losing weight. "If only I could lose 20 pounds," she explained, "my marriage would be so much better."

"What do you mean by that?" the therapist pressed. "How would losing 20 pounds improve your marriage?"

She looked embarrassed, but finally the woman said, "Then my husband would no longer call me 'lazy.'"

Even though it was fairly obvious that the problems she was experiencing in her marriage were hardly connected exclusively to her weight and were far more likely the result of dysfunctional patterns in the couple's communication, the therapist accepted the client's initial definition of the problem at face value—at least until such time that an alliance could be formed. It is often a good therapeutic policy to avoid challenging clients' inaccurate conceptions of their problems too early.

The therapist and client together worked out a structured program in which she worked out for 10 minutes each day on a treadmill. Previously she had followed each "workout" by having a Pepsi that had the same amount of calories that she had just burned off on the treadmill. Clearly, there were some adjustments she would need to make in her eating habits as well (such as switching from a Pepsi to a Diet Pepsi or water). Over the course of several weeks she was able to make these changes, as well as to gradually increase her daily workouts to 40 minutes. Initially, she had to couch her goals around showing her husband her good intentions to lose weight, but as she made progress her goals became more individual around her own ability to maintain her new healthy lifestyle.

Eventually, of course, her loss of the 20 pounds changed very little in the way the couple related to one another. Instead of calling his wife "lazy," the husband just ridiculed her in another way. The next step was to get both partners into joint therapy for some couples work that would more directly intervene at a deeper level. This could not have happened earlier in the treatment until such time as it had already been "proven" that losing 20 pounds would not really fix the problem (although it did wonders for the woman's self-image and confidence).

It is important to note that each of the four stages of Adlerian psychotherapy has its own unique focus, and the therapist does not necessarily follow each one in a sequential fashion. The relationship, assessment, insight, and reorientation stages occur over and over again. The relationship is ongoing in the therapy process, while the assessment begins when the client makes the initial contact with the therapist or enters the therapist's office. Insight and reorientation can occur at any time. Once, a client was filling out the intake forms and then got up and said that by filling out the forms he could clearly see his problem now and knew what he needed to do. He said he would schedule an appointment if it didn't work out. Another client began the session talking about *his* children as his wife listened and the therapist asked if *his* children were from a different marriage. The father looked at the therapist and said no, they are *our* children. The therapist smiled and the wife began to nod her head as the therapist asked her if she felt differently when he said "our" children than when he said "his" children? In this case, the intervention took place in the opening part of the therapy. The steps are more or less sequential, but any stage can effectively appear at different steps of the treatment process.

SELECTIVE ADLERIAN THERAPEUTIC STRATEGIES

Within the stages and therapist roles that have just been described, there are also several unique techniques that are employed. On first glance it might seem like many of these interventions' standards are well-known among those that do clinical work. One of the reasons is that Adlerians have pioneered a wide range of interviews and clinical frames, and many of these methods have been borrowed by other approaches, just as contemporary Adlerian therapists use strategies from compatible systems. Watts and LaGuardia (2015) indicated that most techniques are compatible with Adlerian theory because they originally came from Adler. Corey (2016) added,

> A study of contemporary counseling theories reveals that many of Adler's notions have reappeared in these modern approaches with different nomenclature, and often without giving Adler the credit that is due him. . . . It is clear that there are significant linkages of Adlerian theory with most present-day theories. (p. 126)

In their book *Tactics in Counseling and Psychotherapy*, Adlerian psychologists Harold Mosak and Michael Maniacci (1998) identified 19 different types of tactics that can be used in psychotherapy. These techniques and tactics involve confrontation, motivation, paradox, encouragement, dreams, humor, and change. Highlighted below are some of the ones that are uniquely Adlerian. Some are for individuals while others are better for couples.

Reframing

This is a process of helping a client see the same thing from a different perspective. It is commonly used by therapists across a wide range of theoretical orientations. For the Adlerian therapist, the intervention is aimed at helping people to understand that *everything can really be something else,* and it reflects the notion that one's reality has a subjective perspective to it.

The therapist might say to a despondent client, "It seems like your wife doesn't love you because she has been working overtime to get away from you. I wonder if there's another way to look at this?"

"What are you saying?" the client responds, confused by the challenge.

"I'm just suggesting that there might be other reasons why your wife is not as available as you would prefer—and that this might not necessarily be related to avoiding you, or not loving you."

"You mean, like, to earn more money?"

"Exactly! You've said before that you have complained to your wife about the financial pressure you are under. Isn't it just possible that another reason she is working all those extra hours is because she does love you and wants to help financially as much as she can?"

Clients can be helped to look at their situations in more positive ways.

The Question

Often used in the initial interview, "the question" is used to determine whether a problem is primarily physiological or psychological (Carlson et al., 2006). Also, the question is used to determine whether the client is obtaining special treatment or attention from others for having problems, or which life task is being affected (Mosak & Maniacci, 1998). The therapist asks, "What would be different if your problem were gone?" This is similar to the "miracle question" that is used in solution-focused approaches. The question might be phrased more specifically to a client who has a substance-abuse problem: "How would your life be different if you did not abuse drugs daily?" The answer will help to determine an area of treatment. The client might say, "Then I would have a good job and somewhere to go." The therapist then realizes that intervention is needed in the work task, and in order to break up the pattern of substance abuse, the therapist must help the client find somewhere to go each day that has meaning for the client.

The Push-Button Technique

This imagery technique is used to highlight the control that clients can have over their emotions. It is based on the notion that behind each feeling there is an underlying cognition. Simply stated, if a client can change the cognition and what one is thinking about, then the client can change the emotional reaction. Clients are asked to remember a pleasant experience and then an unpleasant one. The therapist helps clients to realize that they act and think one way in one situation and a different way in another. It goes like this:

Therapist: I'd like you to imagine that you have two buttons on your chest. One button is for each of two different responses. Now picture that however you might respond in any situation, you actually have a choice to push another button and respond in a very different way. These buttons belong to you. Only you can push them. Only you can choose how you want to respond.

(For Antonio, the push-button technique was used to help him learn to respond differently when at work.)

Antonio: I just get so angry at work when I am criticized or not included.

Therapist: Yet there are other times, like at church, when you are really calm and focused.

Antonio: Yeah, but what does that have to do with anything?

Therapist: Can you imagine having two imaginary buttons on your chest? One button tells you to act like you do at work and the other button makes you act like you do at church.

Antonio: Okay, that's funny, but yes I can certainly picture that.

Therapist: So can you imagine yourself at work and instead of pushing the work button, you push the church button? Remember you know how to do both.

Antonio: So you want me to act like I do at church when I'm at work?

Therapist: What do you think would happen if you did that?

Antonio: I would probably get along better with everybody at work, and then work might not bother me so much.

Acting "As If"

Adler was significantly influenced by Hans Vaihinger's (1924) book, *The Philosophy of "As If."* From Vaihinger came the notion that subjective-thought constructs could serve as useful coping tools, namely, that people have a choice in how they can feel and behave. Adler believed that people create cognitive maps that serve as guides for how to lead one's life. Of course, these maps are fictions or constructs that may or may not resemble reality; rather, they are modeled in line with each person's subjective view of the world (Carlson et al., 2006). People act "as if" these maps are real and then live their lives accordingly. The acting "as if" intervention essentially asks the client to try living their life or modeling their behavior in accordance with a different map. This involves suggesting to clients that they act "as if" they didn't have the problem for a week or two (a new map that is not associated with the problem). This pretend exercise allows clients to take actions that previously would have seemed outside the realm of possibility based on their map. An example of this follows.

"For this week," the therapist might say, "I want you to act *as if* you are a good employee. I know that is not the way you have seen yourself until now, nor the way you have been viewed by many others. But just as an experiment, I'd like you to pretend that you really are a good worker. What would that mean?"

The client shrugs.

"Well, how do good employees behave? How do you know one when you see one?" (This is where the therapist is helping the client to envision and create a new map.)

"I don't know. I guess they show up on time, for one."

"Good! What else?"

"They seem happy. They do what they're told."

"What else?"

"I guess most of all they don't have to be told what to do; they just do it on their own."

Now the client knows how to "pretend" to be a good worker, to try on this role to see how it fits.

For Antonio, one of his key concerns was the class difference he constantly felt in his life. He was aware of class differences between his working-class background and his wife's more affluent background. He was also aware of living in a predominately wealthy town with a White majority. He was encouraged to use the acting "as if" strategy.

Therapist: You have mentioned that you feel out of place around Rosa's family, as they are better than you. You also mentioned that you live in a wealthy White community and are not sure if people accept you.

Antonio: That is accurate. That is how it is.

Therapist: I wonder what would happen if the next time you are around Rosa's family, you would be willing to do something different.

Antonio: Well, I do get pretty bored around them, so I might as well have some mission to accomplish when they are around—and her parents are coming next week for a 2-week visit . . . so there's my chance.

Therapist: Would you be willing to act "as if" they saw you as an equal? Act just like you would when you were around your grandfather.

Antonio: That would be weird, but I would try it if you think it might help.

Therapist: Okay, so how did you act and feel around your grandfather?

Another version of the "as if" technique is to ask clients to act as if they can do something they fear, such as speaking confidently or being around snakes (Watts, Peluso, & Lewis, 2005). The rationale is that when clients begin to act differently, regardless of their level of confidence, they tend to become more confident of their abilities, and their beliefs about their abilities also shift. This technique can be expanded to include encouragement to instill inspiration and confidence by asking clients to imagine how their lives would be more positive if they were acting "as if" and then by collaborating to choose behaviors that could increase the likelihood of success in acting "as if" (Watts et al., 2005).

Encouragement

Adlerian therapy is viewed overall as a process of encouragement (Watts, 2012). Clients are not ill or sick; they are discouraged and need encouragement. *Encouragement* means to build "courage" in your client. Courage occurs when people become aware of their strengths, value who they are, feel they belong, and have hope (Carns & Carns, 2006). "I really liked the way you took time this week to read the meditation book. Spend 20 minutes each day in meditation, and drink water in place of alcohol. You have made great progress on your goal of being a more relaxed person." The therapist tells the client exactly what they did that was positive so that in the future they can do their own self-evaluation.

For Antonio, encouragement was crucial because he talked as though he had a low opinion of himself. He seldom felt much ownership of any accomplishments in his life, and he struggled to feel that he was worthy.

Therapist: I listen to you tell me that you are not very successful at work.

Antonio: I don't think that I am.

Therapist: I know that they have let many people go over the last 6 years and yet you have been there for 8 years and are not worried about being terminated. You must be doing something right.

Antonio: I guess that I do okay work. At least I get things done on time.

Therapist: It sounds like you are reliable, dependable, and responsible? Those are impressive qualities.

Antonio: I guess I am, but it is hard for me to see.

Midas Technique

This strategy involves exaggerating the client's neurotic demands. Just like the Greek myth of King Midas, who got his wish and could turn everything into gold, exaggeration allows a client to laugh at their own position. A client who was busy collecting and investing in material wealth was shocked when the therapist suggested that he buy several more burial plots so that he could take all of his possessions with him into the next life. Then he laughed, "Yeah, I see what you mean. I act like I think I'm going to take it all with me. Maybe I should focus more on enjoying and living rather than getting." When a client who seems to be thinking in their usual manner is discussing an upcoming vacation and has way too many activities planned, the therapist might ask with a slight grin, "Can't you do a few more things like bike riding, canoe rental, or maybe rent a Jet Ski between 2:15 and 2:50 on Tuesday?" The client can laugh and understand that he is again overfunctioning. To approach either of these problems with direct questions such as, "Do you think you are too focused on your assets?" or "Do you think you are trying to do too much on your vacation?" would likely meet with resistance.

Pleasing Someone

The therapist urges the client to do something nice for someone else, an act of grace, a *mitzvah*, or a loving gesture. This technique is based on the importance of creating social interest in clients, to reach out beyond their own suffering to help others.

Sometimes clients, especially those in the throes of depression and despair, spend way too much time obsessing about their own situations. They think about themselves constantly, ruminate about the same things, and remain stuck in their "selfness." Such individuals might be encouraged to volunteer their time in service to others, or to make a point of doing something nice for someone every day, with no expectation of a reciprocal favor. Generosity, according to Harvard psychologist Daniel Gilbert (2006), is what leads to happiness.

Avoiding the Tar Baby

This is a strategy to avoid supporting the client's self-defeating behaviors, and the title refers to the notion of a difficult problem or sticky situation that is only aggravated by additional involvement or attempts to solve it. The goal is to act in ways that no longer support the client's negative self-perceptions. The client who claims to dislike other people might be asked to help a friend move, pick up a neighbor's newspaper and take it to the door, or ask an elderly neighbor if she needs anything from the store. The client who "hates people" is acting in ways that oppose the dominant self-perception. In other words, if you behave in ways that are counter to your dominant self-image, dissonance occurs, then that perception begins to change.

For Antonio, it was important to help him understand his lifestyle and how he tended to create situations in which he could have an unfair life. Whereas the therapist explored with Antonio how prejudice and discrimination clearly could contribute to situations of inequity and feeling oppressed, it also appeared that Antonio had developed a pattern of primarily filtering negative perception and information about his life and his difficulties. By expecting the negative and only considering self-defeating information, Antonio was helping to create situations where the outcome always seemed to be bad for him. To begin to combat this, the therapist then helped Antonio learn to construct situations where this would no longer be true and behave in ways contrary to his self-defeating patterns; thus, he could "avoid the tar baby."

Therapist: Your lifestyle assessment seems to say that you are unconsciously creating situations where you end up on the losing end. For example, you get angry at work, which keeps others from seeing your many gifts. At home you tend to let Rosa do too much, which leaves you feeling unneeded.

Antonio: I guess that is true, but I never really understood that before.

Therapist: Let's see if we can think of some ways where you act differently, where everything does not lead to things seeming to be worse for you. Do you have any ideas?

Antonio: I could talk to Rosa and find some things that I can do each day that are helpful. I know I could cook dinner each night and do the laundry. I actually enjoy giving Jorge a bath.

Therapist: Those are just the things I am talking about. When can you start?

Paradoxical Intention or "Spitting in the Soup"

Adler discussed using paradoxical intention with clients. A *paradoxical intention* involves the deliberate practice of a habit or thought to help the client identify and remove it (Carlson et al., 2006). The technique is used to show how clients create their own symptoms—unconsciously—and use them for some purpose. The intervention is the process of the therapist taking an unexpected position of joining clients in their ineffective behaviors that support their symptoms, rather than trying to encourage them to change. A paradox is created in order to stop a client from doing a self-destructive behavior that otherwise has been resistant to change. The therapist prescribes the symptom they are trying to remove in a reverse psychology sort of way. The client can keep doing it, but it feels different since it is something that is allowed or sanctioned. Through this process, clients will often become more aware of how unconstructive the behavior is and stop putting effort into continuing it. The client can still eat the soup; it looks the same, but by spitting in it the therapist takes away the enjoyment or changes the dynamics. For example, Jackson indicated that he was very busy with work and didn't really have time to go on a date with Mandy, his partner of 12 years. The therapist indicated that he had always learned that marriages require regular positive time spent together, but maybe that wasn't really true. He said that Jackson should continue to treat work as the most important thing and not waste time having fun with Mandy. He was sure Mandy would agree that she wasn't that important.

Adlerian or Metta Meditation

The practice of meditation is not new to Adlerian therapy (Hanna, 1996; McBrien, 2004). Hanna (1996) endorsed the introduction of meditation into therapy to encourage the development of social interest. Even though meditating is limited in promoting active social interest, the practice could help a client delve into empathic experiences that are often not addressed in conventional therapies. Carlson (2015b) suggested that Adlerian meditation could adopt a loving-kindness, or *metta*, approach (Carlson, Englar-Carlson, & Emavardhana, 2011) that focuses on kindness and friendliness toward others that one feels in one's heart. Adlerian or metta meditation allows people to cultivate compassion and develop empathy for others by deeply recognizing their inner experience. This process also creates self-control and helps to better understand one's role in relationships (Carlson, 2015b).

The process begins with deep breaths and a focus on yourself. The therapist could instruct as follows:

> As you sit comfortably and begin to focus on your breath, create a clear picture of yourself. It's as if you are sitting across from yourself watching as you relax and breathe. Once you have a clear picture of the self in front of you, say, "May I be peaceful, happy, safe, and free from suffering." Again, to the self in front of you: "May you be peaceful, happy, safe, and free from suffering."
>
> Now move on to picture someone close to you (like your partner, children, parents, friends) sitting in front of you and say to this person, "May you be peaceful, happy, safe, and free from suffering." When you're ready, move on to another person close to you and repeat the process until you have blessed all those close to you.
>
> Next, move on to imagining the people who you see but seldom notice. Those who serve your food and beverage, ride with you on elevators, and those who you briefly interact with each day. Picture each person and wish that they "be peaceful, happy, safe, and free from suffering."
>
> Finally, picture someone with whom you have a conflict or disagreement or simply do not like. Picture this person and say, "May you be peaceful, happy, safe, and free from suffering." Do this practice each day.

Imago Dialogue

The *Imago dialogue* utilized in Imago relationship therapy is a skill that promotes connection, empathy, and horizontal relationships between couples. Adler discussed the need for equality but did not provide a means for this to occur in therapeutic relationships. The Imago dialogue is a means to promote equality and empathy between a couple. The three-part process of mirroring, validating the other, and empathizing is used to create equality (Hendrix, Hunt, Luquet, & Carlson, 2015).

The process is similar to *active listening*, in which the couples take turns listening and sending messages. Couples can quickly learn to see problematic situations from a different perspective and validate one another's viewpoints.

Five Steps to Never Be Lonely Again

Love and Carlson (2011) modified the basic life tasks of Adler into a five-step approach to address loneliness. These five steps are focused on increasing happiness and contentment.

- *Step 1.* Figure out who you are. This is Adler's *self task*. List three characteristics that represent your core values—the attributes that make you "you." Once you have listed the core values for which you stand, begin each day with a commitment to practice these core values. If you are a kind person, make sure you exhibit an act of kindness every single day. Acting out your core values makes you feel congruence with your inner and outer self, and that authenticity will most likely draw others to you.
- *Step 2.* Invest in connections to other people. This is Adler's *social* or *other task*. Most people need about three to five people in their close circle of support, which grows stronger as they invest time, money, and energy. Connecting through technology doesn't count; contact must be face-to-face. Dedicated focus on building support through contact can help increase social interest and connection.
- *Step 3.* Get involved in your community—globally or locally. This is at the heart of *social interest.* Investing time, money, and energy into people outside your social circle can drive away loneliness.
- *Step 4.* Channel your talents into meaningful work. This is Adler's *work task.* You don't necessarily have to get paid for it, but make use of your talents in a way that makes you and/or others feel good about you. This can mean volunteering or engaging in activities that contribute to the social welfare in the local community.

- *Step 5.* Take time to figure out the purpose of your life. This relates to Adler's *task to find meaning in life.* Make sure your everyday habits are representative of your life purpose.

Once you live your core values, strengthen your connections, invest in your community, and apply your talents to meaningful work, you will be living a life of purpose and will never again be lonely.

Taking Ownership

In this couples therapy technique, the therapist encourages a shift in thinking about what the other person is doing in order to focus more on the personal role each person has in the relationship's dynamics. Each accepts responsibility rather than placing blame (Carlson & Lorelle, 2016b).

There are several ways that therapists can encourage couples to take ownership. The therapist should provide psychoeducation about the change process. They introduce the idea that each person will need to look at themself during this process, instead of attempting to change their partner. It is impossible to change anyone else. Metaphors using the idea of teamwork, such as pairs volleyball, skating, or dancing, help to illustrate the concept that it takes effort from both people to be successful. Carlson and Dinkmeyer (2003) described how accepting responsibility for personal behavior and acknowledging this power to make different choices is a first step in improving marriage satisfaction. Assigning a homework reading, such as the first chapter in *Time for a Better Marriage* (Carlson & Dinkmeyer, 2003), reinforces these concepts.

Daily Dialogue

To build deeper connection, the therapist asks a couple to commit 10 minutes each day to a "daily dialogue." During this time, each partner shares for 5 minutes while the other person listens. The topic of these discussions should not be facts about the day's events but, rather, each individual's feelings, including their hopes, fears, insecurities, anger, sadness, or joy. It is important for each person to share insights and reflections about themselves. This is not a time to complain or air gripes about the other partner (Carlson & Dinkmeyer, 2003). Couples often begin by sharing safe or more mundane thoughts and feelings, but with continued dialogue the depth increases.

The listening partner remains silent and practices listening to their partner's feelings and thoughts with an open and nonjudgmental stance. The role of the listener is to seek understanding of what their partner has shared. It may be tempting to argue or contradict what a partner has shared if the other partner disagrees. However, the goal is not to agree with what their partner is saying, but to accept their partner's thoughts, feelings and perspectives as valid, even if they differ from their own (Carlson & Dinkmeyer, 2003). It is important to avoid criticism, attacks, or defensiveness during these discussions. It is best if the partner does not respond or ask questions and instead concentrates on understanding how the thoughts and feelings are true. If someone does not really understand what their partner is expressing, ask for clarification in the therapy session or at a different time (Carlson & Lorelle, 2016a).

Encouragement Meeting

These meetings are held by a couple to strengthen their relationship (Carlson & Dinkmeyer, 2003). The purpose of the encouragement meeting is to allow each partner to share the positive things they are seeing in each other and in the relationship. One partner begins by saying, "The most positive thing that happened today was. . . ." Then the partner continues by saying, "Something I appreciate about you today was. . . ." Then they switch and let the other partner answer the same two questions.

Encouraging Days

List seven to 10 small, pleasant behaviors that your partner can do that will please you. Behaviors should be specific, positive, and unrelated to past conflicts between you. Choose behaviors that are possible for your partner to do on a daily basis. Exchange lists with your partner and strive to do two encouraging behaviors each day (Carlson & Dinkmeyer, 2003).

Marriage Meeting

Meet at a regularly scheduled time when you will not be interrupted. Allow time for a weekly meeting of no more than 45 minutes. Prepare an agenda for the meeting and stick to it. As conflicts or items come up during the week that cannot be quickly resolved, add them to the agenda for the next marriage meeting (Carlson & Dinkmeyer, 2003).

The Four-Step Conflict Resolution Process

Conflict is an inevitable and necessary part of life. The major areas of conflict in marriage are money, sex, work, children, in-laws, religion, friends, substance abuse, and recreation. A four-step process (Carlson & Dinkmeyer, 2003) works effectively:

- *Step 1.* Show mutual respect. Rather than the issue itself, the attitude of one or both partners is often at the heart of the conflict. In a relationship with mutual respect, each partner seeks to understand and respect the other person's point of view.
- *Step 2.* Pinpoint the real issue. Most couples have difficulty identifying the real issue. Concerns usually center on one of the following: you are feeling a threat to your status or prestige, you feel your superiority is being challenged, you need to control or your right to decide is at stake, you feel your judgment is not being considered and you are being treated unfairly, or you feel hurt and need to retaliate or get even.
- *Step 3.* Seek areas of agreement. Concentrate on what you are willing to do, and make no demands that your partner change.
- *Step 4.* Mutually participate in decisions.

Relationship/Marriage Mission Statement

In a couple relationship, there are three parties or entities: you, the other partner, and us. Partners often have conflict because they forget to make the decisions that are best for "us" as they are too busy lobbying for their own position. To effectively put the emphasis on "us" it is important to have a clear statement about who we are and what the purpose or mission of our togetherness is. A relationship/marriage mission statement (Carlson & Dinkmeyer, 2003) expresses what you believe, want, support, and value as a couple. It consists of four parts: (a) desired characteristics of the couple, (b) desired effect upon each partner, (c) meaningful purpose of the relationship, and (d) a clear identification of the source of power or what is important to us (principles). The statement should address issues such as sex, time, sharing, children, support, communication, growth/change, goal/future vision, level of involvement with each other, level of involvement with friends, level of involvement with career, and spiritual issues.

A SECOND ADLERIAN PSYCHOTHERAPY CASE EXAMPLE

Mona was a 41-year-old African American woman who sought out therapy for "mental and spiritual healing." When asked what that meant to her, she explained that she needed to let go of resentment and bitterness toward her husband. She and her husband, Maxwell, had been married for 14 years with two sons, ages 9 and 12. She described herself as unhappy and wanting a divorce, but only if she could be sure the children wouldn't blame her for the divorce. The therapist learned that Mona had met another man at her night college classes and was having an affair. Upon further discussion, Mona revealed that she has had three other affairs since she got married. She wanted to end her marriage, but she felt that she could not hurt her sons, who seemed devoted and loving to their father.

In terms of her own family constellation, Mona reported that she was the fourth of seven children, all girls. Her father left when she was 6 years old, and she and her sisters were raised by their mother in a Chicago public-housing building. Her mother had to work several jobs to support the family, leaving the older children to raise the younger ones in a female-only setting. Mona attended a local inner-city public school, where she was a dedicated and motivated student. She believed that her education made it possible for her to "escape" the city into the suburbs. After high school, she met Maxwell. They dated for a few years before getting married in their mid-20s, and her two boys followed shortly afterward.

Mona worked as a secretary in a law firm and provided the majority of the family income. She was proud of her job and her work history, which showed a steady progression. Mona was upset with Maxwell because he had "settled" for a factory job and his career was stagnant. Maxwell, according to Mona, was dependable, came home after work, attended church, and coached several of the boys' athletic teams. She saw him as happy with his life and not really desiring more out of it. On the other hand, Mona was pursuing her own goals, and was proud that she had completed over 30 credit hours toward a college degree. Her main social connections were with her sisters, her mom, and the church community.

On the lifestyle inventory (see the Appendix), Mona reported that she found her place in her family of origin by being considerate, punished least, sensitive and easily hurt, and having the best behavior. She reported being the most different from her oldest sister, whom she saw as "full of pride and very conceited." Her older sister bragged to make herself feel better, and put down everyone to "light her own fire." Mona reported being most similar to her second-oldest sibling. "She is very smart and laid-back. She accepts less than she deserves."

She reported that her father was "a hard worker and unfaithful, while Mom has never hurt anyone and always does the right thing." Mona views herself as most like her father. When asked in what ways, she stated, "Infidelity and always feeling a need to have someone to lean on."

Mona provided the following early recollections:

- *Early recollection 1.* "I was about 4 years old, and I remember I had a favorite flowered glass I loved to drink out of. One day I climbed on top of the counter to get my glass out of the cabinet and I slipped and fell off the counter and hit my elbow on the floor and broke it. The only thing I remember was that I was in pain and then my mom took me to get a cast."
- *Early recollection 2.* "I was about 8 years old, and my sister and I were playing softball outside with friends and I swung the bat backwards

before I swung it forward and I hit her in the head. I remember feeling so guilty and sorry and just trying to help her up. A knot appeared so quick and I just wanted to make sure she was okay. We (my friends and me) got her upstairs to mom so mom could take a look at her and she ended up okay but the game was over."

- *Early recollection 3.* "I was 7 years old when my mom and sisters moved away from dad and moved into an apartment. I remember the apartment seeming so huge and upon walking in you could hear the echo when talking loud. I was in the living room when my sister hid around the corner making sounds to scare me and anybody else; it worked on me. I remember feeling scared even though other people were in the house, but it didn't last long because mom made her stop."

The lifestyle described a dependent woman who was afraid to make decisions because when she did she and others got hurt. She believed she couldn't take care of herself and needed others to help her. She was a religious person who was afraid of not "doing what is right." She was very close to her mother and sisters, and found living in a "man's world" a bit challenging and foreign.

The therapist supplemented the lifestyle information with another question to better understand Mona as well as to communicate that he wanted to understand her in the context of her world.

Therapist: Who are three people I need to know in order to really know you?

Mona: My mom for sure. She is responsible, loving, a good listener, and saved.

Therapist: Does "saved" mean that she lives her faith?

Mona: Exactly. My friend Wanda is another person you should know. She is saved and good to talk with and my friend Glenda is another who is saved and fun to talk with.

Therapist: It sounds like practicing your faith and good communication are important to you.

Mona: I am a God-fearing woman and as you can probably tell, I love to talk.

Therapist: How do these two things play out in your marriage to Maxwell?

Mona: He is a good Christian man and goes to church and stuff, but he is too quiet.

Therapist: So he is a good man and lets you talk?

Mona: I never looked at it that way, but I guess you're right.

Therapist: Are you a good listener when he talks?

Mona: He is so boring and we have nothing in common but the kids, so what's there to listen to?

Therapist: So what stops you from a divorce?

Mona: Money. I can't afford a lawyer and don't qualify for a pro bono one, and I'm too embarrassed to ask the law partners I work for to help me.

Therapist: Is there anything other than money standing in your way?

Mona: My mother and several sisters have done it, so it isn't a family thing. . . . As I said earlier, I don't want to hurt my children.

Therapist: How do you, a person who tries to do the right thing, justify a divorce?

Mona: I guess that's another problem.

Therapist: A problem for you?

Mona: Not a problem for anyone else, just for me. This is something that I want to do but at the same time cannot seem to do it.

Therapist: Earlier you provided some early recollections that seemed to describe you as someone who doesn't believe she makes good decisions. What makes divorce a good decision for you? How will your life be different?

Mona: I'll be happy.

Therapist: You'll be happy because?

Mona: I won't have to be around Maxwell.

Therapist: Are you around him a lot now?

Mona: Actually I try to never be around him.

Therapist: Are you happy then?

This line of questioning helped Mona realize that she was acting a lot like her selfish older sister and not thinking of her husband's or sons' best interests. She confessed that she really had no idea how to maintain a satisfying relationship with a man. All her affairs started out great, but soon fizzled out, and they all seemed to resemble each other, leaving her feeling unhappy.

The therapist was able to create a safe environment for Mona. The questions provided structure to help her look at her decisions, values, fears, and motivations. The lifestyle information made it possible to isolate some of the faulty thinking that was involved in Mona's plans and decisions. She gained important insight into understanding how her selfish ways were impacting her husband and sons. Thinking that she deserved happiness meant going out to the bars with other men rather than appreciating the happiness she already had being a family with Maxwell and the boys.

Mona agreed to ask Maxwell if he would do a "daily dialogue," which, as stated previously, involves one person talking uninterrupted for 5 minutes while the other listens. At the end of 5 minutes they reverse roles. They are to talk about hopes, joys, fears, sorrows, and anything else they want their partner to know. They are not to respond to one another but just listen.

In the second session, Mona returned claiming to be getting more confused. She indicated that she and Maxwell "daily dialogued" on three occasions, and she learned that he actually had a lot to say that was worth listening to. Maxwell talked about the boys and his thoughts on parenting, what he enjoyed each day and why, and also his appreciation for Mona and God.

She indicated she was hoping the therapist would tell her what to do so she could get on with her life rather than making it more complex and confusing. Mona was having a difficult time making decisions by herself, believing they were not going to work. She wanted a professional to depend on and to tell her what to do.

Therapist: I get the feeling that you would like me to tell you what to do and if I do that I'd be telling you that I agree that you make bad decisions.

Mona: No, I won't think that, really.

Therapist: I have heard of the many good decisions you make and believe you can figure out the right decision.

Mona: What good decisions have I made?

Therapist: For one, you are able to ask for and seek out help. You are resourceful, go to school, and have created a nice house for your boys. You maintain a good job while growing yourself by going to school. You are dedicated to your faith and you consistently make choices to place faith as a critical factor in your family life. . . . Do I need to continue?

Mona: You made your point.

Therapist: Which is?

Mona: I think I make bad decisions (smiling), but in reality I seem to be making some pretty darn good ones.

The therapist helped Mona to see that she had actually become an independent and successful adult in spite of her perceived unhappiness. She was starting to understand her role in her marital unhappiness and realizing that she had no idea how to restore love to her life other than having affairs or divorcing like her parents did. She had a strong Christian faith and conscience that seemed to "torment" rather than comfort her. She felt guilty for affairs as well as her contemptuous treatment of Maxwell, and worried that her actions might be having an effect on her sons.

The therapist suggested that because neither Mona nor Maxwell had models of good marriage relationships, they might benefit from attending a marriage enrichment class. Whether they divorced or stayed together, they needed some education on what makes a relationship successful as well as some skill training. He suggested that Mona look at the Smart Marriages and Happy Families website (http://www.smartmarriages.com) and explore possible classes, several of which are Christian based. Mona loved this idea and was sure that Maxwell also would. Mona was told to contact the therapist once they completed the training.

Western approaches to psychotherapy have traditionally prescribed regular or ongoing meetings where change takes place with a therapist present. Adlerian and more Eastern-influenced approaches to helping hold that learning can occur by training and completing activities without the therapist needing to be present. Mona was able to understand herself and take responsibility for her role in her life's problems. A focused structured intervention that followed the four steps of relationship, assessment, insight, and reorientation had occurred.

A few months later, Mona contacted the therapist and indicated that they had completed the marriage-enrichment class. She stated that she had not yet made a decision but that things were much better with Maxwell, and she had broken off the affair and was no longer seeing the other man. She wanted to thank the therapist and would be in touch, but, at least for now, she needed to keep working on her new relationship skills.

In this brief case, the power of personal engagement and meaningful assessment led to insight and changes in thinking, feeling, and acting. The therapist was active and directive, but mentored within a respectful, equal, and collaborative relationship. In this case, several strategies previously mentioned in this chapter were utilized, including encouragement, reframing, and the question, as well as psychoeducation.

In the next chapter, the evaluation of Adlerian therapy is discussed and the core theoretical concepts presented.

5

Evaluation

Follow your heart but take your brain with you.

—Alfred Adler

This chapter reviews the evidence that supports the myriad of Adlerian concepts and the Adlerian therapeutic approach itself. Even though the Adlerian approach is one of the oldest methods of psychotherapy, the existing empirical base is somewhat limited in comparison with those of many other contemporary models. Due to the fact that so many Adlerian concepts have found their way into models (e.g., cognitive behavioral therapies, reality therapy, solution-focused therapy), we offer the observation that the widespread adoption of Adlerian ideas by other therapies can serve as a positive evaluation of the Adlerian model. Also, the positive evaluation of other approaches serves the function of also validating the Adlerian approach. This suggestion is offered despite the fact that the ability to

http://dx.doi.org/10.1037/0000014-005
Adlerian Psychotherapy, by J. Carlson and M. Englar-Carlson

discriminate effectiveness between different models has not been terribly successful (Luborsky et al., 2002; Miller, Wampold, & Varhely, 2008). Further, Norcross (2002) and a host of contributors have shown that effective practitioners do pretty much the same things regardless of theoretical orientation. In addition, another way to evaluate the Adlerian approach is based on deductive reasoning (Westen, Novotny, & Thompson-Brenner, 2005), by reviewing the work of successful Adlerians in the field. This approach helps provide information about the efficacious application of Adlerian principles and interventions in a variety of settings to improve functioning (Whaley & Davis, 2007).

Below, we review a select range of Adlerian concepts and discuss how contemporary scholars have evaluated the efficacy and application to modern society and clinical practice.

ENCOURAGEMENT

Encouragement is at the core of the Adlerian approach to psychotherapy. Adlerian therapists conceptualize clients as discouraged (i.e., lacking motivation and belief in their abilities to change) rather than ill (Watts & Pietrzak, 2000); thus, the use of encouragement—the antidote to discouragement—is critical to creating therapeutic change. As Main and Boughner (2011) pointed out, encouragement is crucial to the therapist's spirit and presence during therapy and serves as a means to develop social interest on the part of the client (Ansbacher & Ansbacher, 1978). Additionally, it is an actionable approach for the therapist, not a passive attempt to simply encourage hope in the client, but rather the means to inspire "engagement and courage in individuals, children, and families" (Main & Boughner, 2011, p. 270).

In an extensive review on the psychology of encouragement, Wong (2015) noted that in no other approach is encouragement more explicitly emphasized than in the Adlerian approach. His evaluation found that a strength of Adlerian notions of encouragement is the importance placed on building an individual's inner resources, strength, and motivation rather than only trying to modify behavior. That is illustrated by Dreikurs's (1967) observation that Adlerians are in the business of motivation modification, not behavior modification. Wong's review on

Adlerian studies of encouragement noted a lack of consistency across those studies. He observed different meanings within Adlerian scholarship about encouragement, summing it up into two main approaches: *Encouragement* can refer to a social phenomenon or to an individual's way of being. In the first sense, Wong critiqued an inconsistent definition, seeing it defined as inspiring others (Sweeney, 2009), a nonverbal attitude (Nikelly & Dinkmeyer, 1971), and the more common one used by many Adlerians, as "the process of facilitating the development of a persons' inner resources and courage toward positive movement" (Dinkmeyer & Losoncy, 1996, p. 7). In the latter, meaning is more of a humanistic notion that is focused on the psychosocial benefits of encouragement and the notion of being more fully functioning as a person. Studies on these ideas are associated more with a positive view of oneself and being open to experiences (Evans, Dedrick, & Epstein, 1997; Phelps, Tranakos-Howe, Dagley, & Lyn, 2001). This is highlighted by Evans et al.'s (1997) four dimensions of encouragement: (a) a positive view of oneself, (b) a positive view of others, (c) being open to experiences, and (d) a sense of belonging to others.

Drawing on a wide range of thinking about encouragement across psychological disciplines, Wong (2015) evaluated and consolidated previous theorizing and research in proposing an integrative psychology of encouragement that draws heavily on Adlerian concepts (e.g., focus on affirmations to instill courage, perseverance, confidence, inspiration, or hope) to come up with an integrative model of encouragement—the tripartite encouragement model (TEM). The TEM delineates three facets of encouragement processes: foci (challenged-oriented focused on overcoming, or potential-achieving focused on maximizing one's growth), features of effective encouragement (more process-oriented, trustworthy encourager, credible encouragement message), and levels of encouragement (e.g., an act of interpersonal communication, character strength/trait, an ecological group norm). Though the TEM has yet to be tested empirically, it acknowledges the strong role of encouragement in clinical practice and provides guidance for using encouragement to enhance the quality of counseling practice.

Based on a content analysis of encouragement stories taken from over 1,000 racially and internationally diverse people, Eckstein and Cooke

(2005) delineated seven specific methods of influencing through encouragement. These methods were drawn from experiences of people in the past that had provided encouragement. These categories were role models, identifying strengths and weaknesses, consistency of support over the long haul, seeing the person as special, passionate inspiration, supporting a person's special interests, and encouraging career choices. These categories were then developed into a structured interview schedule that couples could use to interview each other. The goal of the interview was for couples to reflect on whom they have encouraged and how they have been encouraged, with the goal of learning how to be a source of encouragement for each other. Eckstein and Cooke suggested that by practicing these seven methods of encouragement and providing opportunities for each other to re-experience moments of past encouragement through reflection, a stronger positive bond can be created between the couple.

Encouragement has also been applied with different populations. Evans (1996) looked at using encouragement to transform classrooms. He reviewed the way three different school programs integrated encouragement in classrooms. Teachers are often trained in stimulus–response techniques that run counter to democratic school-reform principles. Encouragement training, which prioritizes relationships, respectful dialogue, and group decision making, can change the way teachers run their classrooms, resulting in students who are more involved, responsible, and academically successful. Evans noted the importance of encouraging parents, teachers, and classes through different modalities (e.g., letters, classroom meetings), and of using the concept of consequences rather than reward and punishment as a way to create a democratic classroom atmosphere. Other Adlerian scholars have focused on the interpersonal aspect of encouragement in school-age children. For example, a line of research on the distinction between praise and encouragement showed that children rated a teacher's use of encouragement more favorably than a teacher's use of praise (Kelly & Daniels, 1997). Girls often exhibited a higher preference for encouragement versus praise than boys (Pety, Kelly, & Kafafy, 1984). Further, an internal locus of control was related to fourth- and sixth-grade students' preference for encouragement versus praise (Kelly, 2002).

Meunier (1989) explored the use of encouragement group therapy for discouraged elderly residents in nursing homes. The dynamics of using encouragement groups as a form of therapy for socially unconnected and isolated individuals was examined, noting that the goal of such groups is to provide encouragement for the development of social interest in dealing with life tasks. Importantly, the issue of finding new and unique ways to meet life tasks was addressed developmentally, accounting for the process of aging.

Finally, Rowles and Duan (2012) examined encouragement in the face of perceived racism among African Americans. They found a negative relationship between perceived racism and sense of encouragement. Spirituality and ethnic pride positively predicted a sense of encouragement. The negative relationship between perceived racism and encouragement disappeared when spirituality, ethnic pride, and a racial socialization history were entered into the regression equation. In line with aspects of Afrocentric therapies (Phillips, 1990; Williams, 2005), this suggests that Adlerians may need to infuse cultural encouragement that incorporates ethnic pride and spiritual development.

SOCIAL INTEREST

Connected to encouragement, social interest is one of the defining theoretical concepts of Adlerian therapy. *Social interest* refers to one's interest in the welfare of others and a sense of belonging within the human community (Ansbacher, 1992b). Despite the centrality of social interest to Adlerian theory, it can be difficult to define (Bass, Curlette, Kern, & McWilliams, 2002). Some (Stein & Edwards, 1998) have noted that social interest can be expressed on affective, cognitive, and behavioral levels. Ansbacher (1992b) further refined Adler's notion of social interest by observing social interest in two facets: an internal striving to social usefulness, and an external striving toward connection with the community around us. Mental health itself can be measured by one's level of social interest, as Adler (1956) suggested that all failures in life are associated with lower social interest. Accordingly, social interest has been found to be a predictor of happiness (Bass et al., 2002); life satisfaction (Gilman, 2001); empathic concern (Watkins & Blazina, 1994); and the ability to empathize with others, cooperate, and behave in a manner that benefits one's community (Daugherty, Murphy, & Paugh, 2001).

One of the failures in life that Adler highlighted was substance abuse. Many studies (Chaplin & Orlofsky, 1991; Giordano & Cashwell, 2014; Lewis & Watts, 2004) have found an inverse relationship between substance abuse and social interest. Giordano and Cashwell (2014) noted differences in social interest between college students who abused alcohol and marijuana and those that did not. Lewis and Watts (2004) found the quantity of alcohol use to be predicted by social interest. Mozdzierz, Greenblatt, and Murphy (2007) investigated social interest among veterans receiving substance abuse treatment and showed that those with lower levels of social interest had greater alcohol and drug dependence compared with those with more social interest. Social interest has also been examined in relation to substance abuse relapse. Giordano, Clarke, and Furter (2014) studied social interest and social bonding in relation to predicting relapse and found that lower social interest and lower social bonding were predictive of fewer days before relapsing. They suggested that intervention efforts focusing on growing social interest and social bonding in treatment could be more effective in relapse prevention.

Other research has explored the relationship between social interest and coping. Crandall (1984) found that social interest was associated with personal adjustment, observing that social interest reduced the effects of stress on psychological symptoms and could provide some resistance to the effects of stress. Leak and Williams (1991) investigated the connection between social interest and family relationships, with their results indicating that those higher in social interest had more family connectedness and were more open to personal growth. They concluded that social interest "encourages an active approach to life's problems" (p. 374). Kern, Gfroerer, Summers, Curlette, and Matheny (1996) found that social interest and belonging were related to adults' perceived coping resources. In terms of youth, Edwards, Gfroerer, Flowers, and Whitaker (2004) empirically examined the relationship of social interest and coping skills in elementary-school children. They found that through a variety of deliberate activities social interest could be increased, which influenced a child's ability to cope with life demands. Further, the study showed a reciprocal relationship between social interest and belonging, namely, that a child who possesses a high level of social interest also feels a sense of belonging. For young adults, Johnson, Smith, and Nelson (2003) showed that higher levels of family cohesiveness and expressiveness and lower levels of conflict were predictive of the development of social interest in adulthood. Those who perceive themselves as content with their family closeness, who felt comfortable with the expression of warmth and caring by their family, and who resolved differences without blaming and arguing were more likely to exhibit caring and altruism for others and connectedness beyond their family system as emerging adults.

There have also been recent international studies that examined social interest. Alizadeh (2012) discussed the presence of social interest in Islamic texts. Alizadeh described multiple common aspects of social interest and Islam around issues of community, unity, equality, spirituality, and even as a barometer of mental health. Ergüner-Tekinalp and Terzi (2014) investigated social interest in a Turkish sample. Results demonstrated that social interest was significantly related to active planning, seeking external help, turning to religion, and acceptance/cognitive restructuring coping styles. Specifically, individuals who sought external help for coping had higher social interest and thus were more resilient. Social interest was also predictive of psychological hardiness, which has important implications for personal adjustment and well-being. Kim, Park, and Hogge (2015) researched whether the Adlerian notion that both activity and social interest would be related to decreased depression and whether meaning in life would mediate these relationships among Korean retirees. Higher levels of social interest were directly related to lower levels of depression. In addition, meaning in life was an important avenue through which activity and social interest were linked to a lower level of depression among these retirees.

Other scholars have observed the utility of promoting social interest in accordance with changes in modern society. On the basis of her corporate work experience and a range of multicultural life experiences, Uccello

(2009) used social interest as a medium to explore social reasonability in corporate environments. She looked at the impact of global corporations on employees and the environment, and suggested that developing social interest could be a sustainable corporate value. Social interest supports efforts toward social responsibility while empowering employees to view their work and careers in the context of social interest and social responsibility. Two other articles considered social interest in relation to advances in technology and online relationships/communities. Close (2015) questioned whether social interest could be developed in clients through the virtual world of the Internet. These environments support the cognitive development of socially interested thinking, yet growing the somatic communal-sense dimension of social interest as a healing dynamic in an actual relationship may present challenges. Hammond (2015) examined social interest and the related concept of empathy in online support groups. She commented that online socialization and expression of empathy in virtual environments can support the development of social interest while also presenting new avenues for connecting with clients and for clients to connect with and support others in need. Online groups provide many windows for supportive interactions in which social interest can be developed.

Some have located social interest in other therapeutic approaches. McBrien (2004) looked at the psychology of forgiveness and noted the relationship between forgiveness and social interest. Though Adler is rarely cited in the forgiveness literature, McBrien noted many connection points, for example, that the cosmic dimension of social interest (i.e., its spiritual form) helps in understanding the spiritual dimension included in some Christian theories of forgiveness, and that developing social interest as a therapeutic goal applies to forgiveness issues. Specifically, encouraging forgiveness in Adlerian psychotherapy is connected "to a client's willingness to become more understanding, to have more compassion, and to experience empathy for the offender. In Adler's words, this would mean living with social interest" (McBrien, 2004, p. 115).

The Adlerian emphasis as growth and positive-focused psychology has led to many connections between Adlerian psychotherapy and the field of positive psychology (Carlson, Watts, & Maniacci, 2006; Leak & Leak, 2006; Mozdzierz, 2015). Mozdzierz (2015) observed that the operational principles of many of Adler's original concepts (e.g., social interest, encouragement, importance of meaning, focus on health and growth) are clearly relevant in the current discourse with positive psychology. The Adlerian connection to positive psychology is so evident that Mozdzierz (2015) offered the rhetorical question, "What is Positive Psychology?" Adlerians might respond to such a question by asking, "Is there any other kind of psychology?" (p. 362). Leak and Leak integrated social interest with positive psychology. Adler observed that social interest involves a genuine and generous concern for the welfare of others, and that positive mental health requires social interest. Leak and Leak (2006) conducted two studies that supported the idea that social interest was related to numerous aspects of positive psychology (e.g., subjective well-being, other-centered values, prosocial moral reasoning, psychosocial maturity). They found that social interest was positively related to key aspects of healthy functioning championed by positive psychology (e.g., values, traits, motives) and negatively associated with maladaptive functioning. They concluded that social interest could be considered under the umbrella of numerous attributes stressed by positive psychology.

BIRTH ORDER

Birth order is one of the most enduring theoretical Adlerian concepts, and it continues to inform professionals practicing from an Adlerian theoretical perspective (Eckstein & Kaufman, 2012). Research on birth order by Adlerians is robust (Stewart, 2012). At least 200 empirical studies have found some significant differences between the birth orders (Eckstein et al., 2010). The majority of the research on birth order has been conducted to better understand the relationship between family conditions and the well-being of individuals (Heiland, 2009). Despite the large amount of research, methodological issues across studies have led to inconsistent findings and critiques. Hartshorne, Salem-Hartshorne, and Hartshorne (2009) noted one of the main confounds is that there is neither consensus nor rules as to how to rank birth order between disciplines. Most researchers use the Adlerian method of ranking birth order (Mills & Mooney, 2013), that is, with the birth order positions of first-born, middle-born, last-born, and only children. This categorization is helpful because it can distinguish the effects of each position in comparison with the others. It also taps into psychological birth order, as "Adler always placed more emphasis on the person's self-perceived position in the family, as this contributes to ways the child approaches the tasks of completion and belonging" (Stewart, 2012, p. 77). The Adlerian approach is a psychology of use, not possession, and psychological birth order acknowledges that people are not fixed victims of their ordinal birth position; rather, they are able to work with what they have and how they respond to the givens of their birth order within their family constellation. Eckstein et al. (2010) noted that Adlerians use birth order research to help understand some common patterns in families but always fall back on the understanding that personality implications are not one-size-fits-all. These final observations are important to keep in mind as Adlerians use flexibility to interpret birth order and lifestyle experiences with clients.

Eckstein et al. (2010) reviewed 200 published articles with statistically significant findings of birth order characteristics to delineate lifestyle characteristics. Although these studies were a combination of ordinal and psychological birth order investigation, the authors found some common characteristics associated with persons in specific birth order positions. Their review found lifestyle characteristics of high success and achievement for first-born children, high need for achievement for only children, high sociability for middle children, and high social interest for the youngest children.

CULTURAL AND INTERNATIONAL APPLICATIONS

Throughout this book we have highlighted the multicultural aspects of Adlerian theory and the ways that the approach can be modified to account for a wide range of human experiences. *Culturally responsive therapies* are those that access and incorporate clients' cultural meanings or models throughout evaluation and treatment (La Roche & Christopher, 2009; Whaley & Davis, 2007). Many of the core aspects of Adlerian psychotherapy mirror recommendations for effective multicultural psychotherapy. These include the importance of an egalitarian, respectful, and cooperative counselor–client relationship (therapeutic alliance); the focus on social equality and social justice; taking a holistic approach that considers mind, body, and spirit; the need to view people contextually, in their family, social, and cultural contexts; and the emphasis on strengths, optimism, encouragement, empowerment, advocacy, and support.

Adlerian therapy also has a global reach, as the educational principles and practice of psychotherapy are seen throughout much of the world. Sperry and Carlson (2012a, 2012b) edited two volumes of *The Journal of Individual Psychology* (Vol. 68, Nos. 3–4) that examined an international view of Adlerian psychology. These issues serve as an introduction to the spread and diffusion of Adlerian principles and practices in several countries. Importantly, these articles highlight the necessary process of adaptation and accommodation of Adlerian value to match the target culture and context. Sperry and Carlson (2012b) made the point that the global spread of Adlerian concepts is more like a cultural exchange in which the theory has been both assimilated in some countries and accommodated in others to match the host country and culture so that it is culturally appropriate. Thus, the cultural exchange is more akin to a negotiation. They added, "such cultural accommodations without losing the intent of the [theoretical] construct suggest the flexibility and viability of the Adlerian approach" (Sperry & Carlson, 2012b, p. 207). Many of the studies from these special issues are mentioned throughout this book and in this chapter already, but a few additional studies that highlight international applications are reviewed next.

There are multiple accounts of the application of Adlerian theory in Asia. Carlson, Englar-Carlson, and Emavardhana (2011, 2012) reviewed Adlerian concepts in regard to Thailand, with an emphasis on Buddhist influences. They highlighted some commonalities between the Buddhist and Adlerian approaches to life and health, including the interconnectedness of all people; that people both impact and are impacted by their communities, culture, families, and so forth; and that both approaches view people as social animals and place a high value on relationships. A common theme for both is that community striving (i.e., social interest) and harmony bring happiness and good health. Sun and Bitter (2012) explored the application of Adlerian psychology and therapy in Chinese and South Korean cultures. Aspects of collectivist Chinese culture, such as the emphasis on personal-interpersonal relationships and social contact, are conceptually similar to Adlerian theory (e.g., both assert that human growth is accomplished through a productive engagement with others, rather than a decline into self-absorption or living in a self-centered manner) but are viewed as different in actual practice between Western and Chinese standards. The compatibility of Adlerian psychotherapy with Chinese culture was also highlighted in relation to views on human nature, inferiority feeling and the inferiority complex, birth order, and therapeutic relationships. For South Koreans, social interest is similar to *jeong*, which is a combination of empathy, compassion, and emotional attachment in accordance with the social context. Like social interest, it is also central to maintaining human connection and demonstrating concern for others. Sun and Bitter concluded that Adlerian therapy has much in common with the core values of both cultures.

Brack, Hill, Edwards, Grootboom, and Lassiter (2003) reviewed how Adlerian principles have been used to address the psychosocial challenges in South African schools. They discussed social interest in relation to the South African philosophy of Ubuntu. [*Ubuntu* has been described as a philosophy of life, which represents personhood, humanity, humaneness, and morality and serves as a worldview of African societies.] In particular, Ubuntu promotes the notion that a person can only be a person through others, so an individual's whole existence is relative to that of the group. This is similar to the Adlerian notion that people are innately "social creatures" who exist in groups in order to survive and thrive. School counselors integrated Adlerian principles with Ubuntu to address the vast challenges in South Africa associated with decades of racist, sexist, and classist policies. With histories of fragmented communities and schools, growing Ubuntu and social interest among students, staff, and communities seemed like a natural route to begin the healing process.

ADLERIAN THERAPEUTIC APPROACHES

Adlerian psychotherapy does not have the robust psychotherapy outcome evidence base that other forms of therapy have. In Chapter 6, we discuss this in more detail. Certainly, Adlerian scholars see this as an area of future growth. While developing a stronger evidence base for Adlerian psychotherapy core competencies is essential, Sperry (2011) commented that the body of Adlerian psychotherapy theory and method already contains much of the knowledge and skill base for many of the needed competencies. There are many modes in which Adlerian therapy can be delivered. Below, we review some of these Adlerian clinical approaches.

Forms of Adlerian brief therapy have been previously developed (Nicoll, Bitter, Christensen, & Hawes, 2000). Wood (2003) positioned Adlerian psychotherapy as a form of brief therapy that could be 20 sessions or less. Wood noted that from the onset, Adlerian therapy has been time sensitive and shares many of the qualities of other brief therapies, such as being a goal-oriented treatment that draws on client strengths and client–therapist collaboration to quickly accomplish positive change. Sequential brief Adlerian psychodynamic psychotherapy (SB-APP; Ferrero, 2012) is another time-limited (40 sessions) psychotherapy developed for a wide range of presenting concerns delivered in a sequential and repeatable module. A feature of this is that the therapy includes four repeatable modules in which a different therapist is involved in each module. Ferrero and colleagues (2007) compared the effects of brief Adlerian psychodynamic psychotherapy (B-APP) with those of (a) pharmacological intervention and (b) a combination of pharmacological intervention and B-APP on clients experiencing generalized anxiety disorder (GAD) over a 6-month period. They found B-APP was an effective therapeutic intervention in the treatment of GAD by itself and in combination with pharmacological treatment. Results indicated a decrease in both anxiety and depressive symptoms, and these changes were stable in a 1-year follow-up session. While a combination of medication and B-APP was found to be the most effective form of treatment, participants who received B-APP did not need continued medication a year later, while those who received medication alone did.

Adlerian play therapy (AdPT) is a well-developed, manualized child-counseling model (Kottman, 2011; Kottman & Ashby, 2015; Kottman & Meany-Walen, 2016) with an abundance of literature describing its theoretical tenets and practical application with elementary-age children. AdPT is one of the top three approaches to play therapy (Lambert et al., 2007). Meany-Walen, Bratton, and Kottman (2014) examined the effective use of

AdPT on elementary students exhibiting disruptive classroom behaviors. Their study demonstrated positive outcomes for children with disruptive classroom behavior who received AdPT with both teachers and outside raters observing a significant reduction in behavioral problems. Further, teachers reported a statistically significant reduction in stress in their relationships with students receiving AdPT. Meany-Walen, Kottman, Bullis, and Dillman Taylor (2015) used a single-case research design to measure the effectiveness of AdPT on the classroom behaviors of six boys. The results showed improvement in the children's behavior during and after the intervention, suggesting again that AdPT is a promising intervention for children's externalizing classroom behaviors. Meany-Walen et al. (2015) further investigated group AdPT to address off-task behaviors. The group format showed on-task behaviors improve during the group play-therapy intervention, yet the long-term assessment revealed mixed findings for the follow-up period.

Adlerians have made some of their greatest impact in the area of parenting education and training. It is worth noting that both *Systematic Training for Effective Parenting* (Dinkmeyer, McKay, & Dinkmeyer, 2008) and *Active Parenting* (http://www.activeparenting.com) are recognized as evidence-based practices. Both of these programs are on the National Registry of Evidence-Based Programs and Practices (http://www.samhsa.gov/nrepp).

SUMMARY

In this chapter, we reviewed some of the evidence that supports Adlerian theoretical concepts. Since so many Adlerian therapeutic concepts and interventions have been co-opted by other approaches, we suggest that, overall, there is a positive assessment of Adlerian psychotherapy. Further, the utility of Adlerian psychotherapy is evidenced by the worldwide application of the approach. The next chapter both critiques the current state of Adlerian psychotherapy and highlights what the future could hold for the theory.

6

Suggestions for Future Developments

Individual Psychology is like a basket of fruit, one which
any passer-by can take whatever agrees with him.

—Phyllis Bottome

Adlerian psychotherapy is fortunate to have a considerable history upon which to reflect. As the reader can ascertain from the previous chapters, Adlerian psychotherapy has been largely associated with the direct work of Alfred Adler. Adler had insight into human development and growth, and his ideas made a lasting impression across the entire field of psychotherapy. Many of the most influential figures in the theory and practice of psychotherapy noted how Adler influenced their thinking and the conceptual development of their own respective approaches (e.g., Albert Ellis, Aaron Beck, William Glasser, Carl Rogers, Victor Frankl, Abraham Maslow, Rollo May; Carlson, Watts, & Maniacci, 2006). Practically every other theory

http://dx.doi.org/10.1037/0000014-006
Adlerian Psychotherapy, by J. Carlson and M. Englar-Carlson

now claims him as a grandparent (e.g., person-centered, reality therapy, constructivist, cognitive, rational emotive, cognitive behavior, integrative, family; Carlson & Johnson, 2009). In Chapter 5, we observed that much of the evidence that supports the efficacy of an Adlerian approach is found in the work of Adlerian scholars and the widespread adoption of Adlerian concepts in other approaches. In that sense, the future of Adlerian psycho-therapy is optimistic due to the strength of the conceptual model. It seems like the basic or essential components of Adler's individual psychology have been utilized by so many of the contemporary approaches that it seems obvious that the comprehensive model would be very well-suited for the practice of psychotherapy. One of the ongoing tasks of all models, however, is to continually evolve and grow to match contemporary trends in modern society and culture, and in the practice of psychotherapy itself. It is the latter—taking Adlerian ideas and continuing to elevate the effi-cacy of the approach among practitioners—where Adlerians face continu-ing challenges.

We offer this chapter as a critique of the existing Adlerian approach and as an opportunity to explore future directions for advancement of the theory. In the first part of the chapter, we review our ideas about the current strengths and challenges that Adlerians face. In the second half, we have invited many prominent Adlerians to offer their own perspectives about future Adlerian developments.

OUR FUTURE CONSIDERATIONS

The Adlerian approach does face some ongoing challenges that are neither new nor insurmountable. Legitimacy in the field of psychology and pro-fessional psychotherapy tends to be attained by having practitioners with advanced training (primarily doctoral level) and empirical scholarship that validates an approach (Wampold, 2010). In many ways this has always been the case, but it is certainly true now more than ever as science and prac-tice have become intertwined (Wampold & Imel, 2015). This is not a bad thing, but for Adlerians it highlights an area of vulnerability in keeping the approach relevant. Very few Adlerians have doctoral degrees and advanced training in psychotherapy. Many Adlerians are drawn to Adler's approach to helping others because it aligns with their own philosophies and goals to make a difference (i.e., social interest) and so they are less interested in theory or research. Many want to help and serve, and thus find that master's level training suffices in being able to engage in direct service. The few Adlerians with advanced training or faculty with doctoral degrees are involved in training laypeople and paraprofessionals in the skills that help others lead more productive lives and not in advancing the Adlerian approach to psychotherapy (Sperry, 2016a). In many ways, Adlerians are like Adler himself—or even Dreikurs, for that matter—in that the desire to work with real people comes first. All of these intentions are positive, but they put the Adlerian approach in a difficult position compared with other approaches that might be more invested in promoting and researching theoretical evidence-based practice. We believe that more research, study, and scholarship of Adlerian psychotherapy are needed, with the specific goal of outlining an Adlerian evidence-based psychotherapy.

Its strong foundation helps Adlerian psychotherapy maintain a healthy theoretical outlook. There are many active Adlerians around the globe who are working together to train future clinicians and academics in the principles and practices of Adlerian psychology. There are two universities (Adler University and Adler Graduate School) devoted to the study of Adlerian principles and clinical training. Two professional organizations exist (North American Society of Adlerian Psychology, and International Association of Individual Psychology) that hold annual conferences and training to engage Adlerians worldwide in scholarly discourse. *The Journal of Individual Psychology* is a highly regarded journal published for over 100 years that is devoted to the research and practice of individual psychology and will continue to enhance the status of the Adlerian movement with the publication of high-quality manuscripts. All of these elements ensure that the model will continue to grow and that Adlerians will have outlets for training, publishing, and interaction.

Adlerian psychotherapy is popular with mental health counselors, whose numbers have been growing with recent changes in licensure. It is also not surprising the Adlerian ideas are well established in the area of school counseling. Adlerians' practical emphasis on parenting, consultation, child development, and developmental guidance reflects the core content areas of school counselors; therefore, many school-based therapists and psychologists are well-grounded in the Adlerian approach. The professional community is recognizing that most contemporary approaches to psychotherapy are Neo-Adlerian and not Neo-Freudian. It is becoming clear that contemporary approaches have used valuable pieces of Adler's complete psychotherapy in their development, thereby mainstreaming Adlerian ideas into contemporary psychological thought and treatment (Mosak & Maniacci, 1999; Mozdzierz & Krauss, 1996). Whether it is positive psychology, cognitive behavioral therapy, family therapy, solution-focused therapy, multicultural therapy, social justice, feminist therapy, or any other, all have claimed a portion of Adler's approach as the hallmark of their own. Adler's complete approach seems to use the key components of many of these other approaches because they were actually part of his original model. These key concepts include the importance of the relationship and the treatment alliance, the core conditions of the therapist, positive psychology, social interest and social justice, the importance of culture and equality, the importance of cognitions, holism, the influence of the family of origin, the importance of the social context, and phenomenology.

Two areas where the Adlerian approach is particularly well-suited for modern practice are its consideration of context and culture in working with clients (Jones-Smith, 2012) and its growth-oriented/strength-based perspective (Carlson et al., 2006; Sapp, 2006). It seems logical that Adlerians could benefit from furthering their professional connections and scholarly links with other professionals in these areas. Many aspects of the positive psychology movement specifically align with Adlerian theory and therapy. Examples include the emphasis on normal human growth and development, prevention/education rather than merely remediation, less of a reliance on the medical model perspective, a focus on mental health and a client's strengths, resources, and abilities rather than psychopathology and a client's disabilities, and the emphasis on encouragement, positive empathy, holism, wellness, multiculturalism, and social justice (Ansbacher & Ansbacher, 1956; Carlson et al., 2006; King & Shelley, 2008; Mosak &

Maniacci, 1999). Whereas Adlerians (Carlson et al., 2006; Watts, 2000b) often note that Adlerian concepts and Adler himself are frequently ignored as important foundational precursors of positive psychology, Adlerians can take a cue from positive psychology and how successful it has been in the past 15 years in creating a robust empirical base.

Adlerian theory's emphases on person-in-environment, sociocultural systems, and culture/context help in understanding clients in a manner that is respectful of individual and cultural identities and heritage (Dagley, 2000; Perkins-Dock, 2005) while also recognizing the influence of con-textual influences upon individuals, communities, and cultural groups (Dufrene, 2011). Psychotherapy needs to account for and adapt to a client's culture (Smith, Rodríguez, & Bernal, 2011), and Adlerians work to inte-grate a client's culture and contextual factors from the onset (Sperry, 2015). Adlerian theory also allows for a culturally relativistic stance in understand-ing psychological deviation. Thus, Adlerian theory can be particularly use-ful in conceptualizing and treating culturally bound syndromes (Miranda & Fraser, 2002), such as the *Hwa-byung* (i.e., the Korean anger syndrome discussed previously that develops as a result of built-up, unresolved, and suppressed anger and other negative feelings; Kim & Hogge, 2013). Taken as a whole, the Adlerian approach is highly conducive to modern concep-tualizations of multicultural counseling, and we believe that Adlerians will continue to become a larger part of the multicultural counseling literature.

One of the reasons why we believe that Adlerians will be efficacious advocates for effective multicultural practice is the model's emphasis on social interest and social justice. Many psychotherapists and graduate stu-dents have increased their commitment to providing multicultural and advocacy-competent therapy to diverse populations, and this has brought issues of diversity and social justice to the forefront (Ratts, Singh, Nassar-McMillan, Butler, & McCullough, 2016; Rubel & Ratts, 2011). The concept of social interest with an emphasis on helping others, belonging, and focus-ing on the collective spirit fits well with and supports the traditional value system of many cultures. Social justice and advocacy are at the core of the graduate training program at Adler University in Chicago. All Adler stu-dents are required to get started on being socially responsible practitioners and "changing the world" by completing a community service practicum in economically challenged communities in Chicago and Vancouver each year that they study. Adler University defines *socially responsible graduates* as people who embrace diverse perspectives; work to build and maintain bridges across social, economic, cultural, racial, and political systems; empower others to identify and address shared problems; and foster the development of social equality, justice, and respect through compassionate action throughout the global community. The key guiding idea is Adler's concept of *social interest*—the idea that our health resides in our community life and connections. Adler advocated wellness in the community context. He advanced the idea that responsible practitioners must advocate to change the social conditions that affect population health and well-being.

Whereas there are clear strengths that will carry the Adlerian approach into the future, we also struggle with what can be done with Adlerian psychotherapy to make sure that it has an important future impact on the world. We recognize that many of the things that our teachers did and that we learned—like lifestyle demonstrations and open-forum sessions—are valuable as educational devices, but these may not reflect what mainstream psychotherapy practices and the market itself demand. Most of Adler's work is reflective of a different era of clinical practice that is not as relevant today. It is more akin to early psychoanalysis or what Henry Stein (Stein & Edwards, 1998) called "classical Adlerian therapy." More effort must be devoted to developing and researching a brief model that treats a client in six to eight 50-minute sessions.

What we have offered thus far as future directions are not necessarily new ideas. Prominent Adlerians (Carlson, 1989, 2000; Huber, 1991; Sperry, 1991; Watkins, 1997) for decades have urged other Adlerians to go "on beyond Adler" (Carlson, 1989) out of concern of being either a "dinosaur or footnote" in psychotherapy history (Carlson, 2000). That admonishment includes updating the model to reflect modern practice and the clinical/societal issues of today (Huber, 1991). Those types of proclamations are made because Adlerians are well aware that there are fewer Adlerian practitioners than before and that other approaches are much more popular. Another concern is that Adlerians are too tied to Adler and unable to grow beyond his vision. Karasu (1992, as cited in Watkins, 1997) noted that any good theory should serve as an anchor; however, it should not so anchor us that we drown. Watkins added, "Sometimes we need to raise anchor, chart new waters, or polish up that which becomes rusty or tarnished over time" (p. 211). Building on the notion, Carlson (2000) observed,

> If Adlerian therapy is to flourish in the new millennium, it will not be limited solely to the work and thinking of one brilliant man. It will represent his core psychological and educational principles, but they will need to continue to be expanded and extended by a new generation of visionaries who not only understand them but are committed to teaching them in the world. (p. 4)

For Adlerians, a successful future involves continuing to use the tools and vision of Adler in a manner that evolves with modern society and psychological science.

PROMINENT ADLERIANS REFLECT ON FUTURE DIRECTIONS

To have a more comprehensive view of the future of Adlerian therapy, as well as to expand our futuristic thinking, we have solicited the thoughts and ideas of several of the leading contemporary voices of Adlerian psychology. We asked each contributor to comment on the future of Adlerian psychotherapy.

Eva Dreikurs Ferguson, a psychologist and daughter of Rudolf Dreikurs, believes that too many therapists focus on immediate symptoms and their relief. The Adlerian approach, however, advocates long-term social-cognitive changes that involve one's sense of "meaning" and "belonging." She believes that Adler's social-evolutionary emphasis will continue to thrive in the future of psychotherapy (Ferguson, 2015).

Roy Kern, editor of *The Journal of Individual Psychology*, believes that Adlerian writers and researchers in the field need to branch out and publish in other recognized scholarly journals in the field. The expansion of publications in other reputable journals will lead to increases in the number of professionals that become more informed about the theory. Kern also sees the need to grow the number of faculty who teach Adlerian ideas so that they can encourage other students. Without a university base, the theory is destined to become a footnote in the history of psychology. Finally, though Adlerians can expound the value of the theory, the wave of the future is evidence-based treatment strategies. For the theory to have any form of impact in the future, there must be more empirically based studies. Books, articles, and monographs related to the application of the theory are available, but there is a true shortage of empirical studies to support the major constructs of the theory (R. Kern, personal communication, July 3, 2015).

Jill Duba Sauerheber, a professor at Western Kentucky University and president of the North American Society of Adlerian Psychology (NASAP), indicates that more and more of our licensed professional helpers are graduating from programs that are not "theoretically pure" (J. Duba, personal communication, July 5, 2015). This is due in part to affiliated professional-education standards and accreditation guidelines that demand a curriculum that incorporates a wide variety of learning and experiential objectives. What does this mean for the future of Adlerian psychology? First, this implies that upcoming generations of Adlerians will come to the table having been exposed to a variety of counseling theories. This knowledge base may nudge them even deeper into Adlerian psychology (because they will find themselves disagreeing with the other theoretical propositions). It may give them the necessary momentum to understand how tenets of other counseling theories can add to and enhance their knowledge and application of Adlerian psychology.

Second, Adlerians must consider that more and more research is available on how mental health professionals should incorporate knowledge about how the brain regulates emotions, thoughts, and physiology. For example, Bridge and Voss's (2014) research in neuroscience about the fluidity of memory and how it changes supports Adlerian theoretical notions about how early recollections work. Many of our new mental health professionals are graduating having been briefed on this information and other new findings. We should heed and listen to them. Attending to and incorporating new information does not mean we are becoming less pure or are betraying our roots. Rather, it implies that we are in tune with the research that has been conducted over time and we are adding it to our depth of and roots in Adlerian psychology. If we want a seat at the table in 2017 and beyond, it is essential that Adlerians do this.

Len Sperry, professor at Florida Atlantic University, describes the need for Adlerians to strive to create research that supports their approach. Evidence-based practice (EBP) does mention the Adlerian-based STEP and Active Parenting programs as EBP, but there are no other mentions of Adlerian therapies. He notes that for clinicians, a main attraction of Adlerian psychotherapy is that it is flexible and fosters an eclectic approach to treatment. Typically, this means that while clinicians find the Adlerian method of assessing lifestyle very helpful, they appreciate that the approach allows them to choose any number of intervention techniques from various therapeutic approaches. However, in this current era of EBP, that positive attribution has become an albatross of sorts for Adlerian psychotherapy. Specifically, while Adlerian psychotherapy is considered strong on assessment (lifestyle assessment: family constellation, early recollections, and lifestyle convictions), it is weak on intervention since it has no unique and defined treatment approach (L. Sperry, personal communication, July 6, 2015).

While a number of contemporary psychotherapy approaches are considered EBPs, Adlerian psychotherapy is not one of them. Adlerian psychotherapy is not considered an evidence-based approach because it has neither articulated a unique intervention method nor provided compelling research data to support its effectiveness. To remain relevant and consistent with the increasing demand for EBP, the theory and practice of Adlerian psychotherapy must be extended to include such an identifiable and unique intervention method or methods. To this end, Sperry has been training therapists in an intervention method that directly focuses on changing what Adlerians refer to as an individual's maladaptive life strategy or pattern. It is called pattern-focused psychotherapy (Sperry, 2016b), but it could just as well be called lifestyle-focused psychotherapy. The future of Adlerian psychotherapy rests on the development of such intervention methods and the research that demonstrates their effectiveness.

Leigh Johnson-Migalski, a faculty member at Adler University, also calls for research on the effectiveness of Adlerian therapeutic interventions. She notes that so much of Adler's theory is revolutionary and relevant today, in terms of women's rights; the need to focus on social context to understand people; concern about inequality among people; and systems that suppress belongingness, health, and significance. She sees Adler's concept of masculine protest as a paradigm to show how a systemic point of view of privilege impacts how people experience marginalization and their self-concept and increases their feelings of inferiority, resulting in various ways of compensation (L. Johnson-Migalski, personal communication, July 9, 2015).

James Sulliman, clinical psychologist and former NASAP president, thinks that to consider the future of Adlerian psychology, it is critical to imagine the future itself. While there are many changes that one could reasonably predict, a brief extrapolation from the past and present suggests a couple of areas that will impact all of psychology's theoretical orientations: (a) the unimaginable (for most) advances in technologies and (b) the lessening influence of religious beliefs in the formation of personal values (J. Sulliman, personal communication, July 15, 2015).

Adlerians have always been teleoanalytic with one eye on the future, often welcoming any change that leads to overcoming obstacles and the betterment of the world. Regarding technology, the challenge will be to maximize the benefits of this tool of unimaginable potential. The same knife that removes cancer in the operating room can be used to slit the throat of the patient in the back alley of the hospital as he is robbed on the way to his vehicle. For Adlerians, it has never been about the gifts we have at our disposal but how we use them—not possession but utilization. It will be just as true in the virtual world with its ever-increasing citizenry as it has been in the real one.

Second, we are witnessing an increased movement away from organized religions, as evidenced by church memberships and active participation reports. As the world becomes more secularized, and "self"-centeredness becomes more the rule rather than the exception, from where will come the values that promote the community, the care for the welfare of others, the principles of healthy relationships? Borrowing essential elements from religions that he saw as universal truths regarding human relationships, Adler included in his therapy model the striving for mastery or "perfection," the creative power of the person, the indivisibility of the individual, that behavior is "purposeful," that man is a social being, and behavior can be useful or useless based on its contribution to growth. Long ago, he declared that "social interest" was "the hope for mankind" if only it were universally practiced. The principles Alfred Adler delineated 100 years ago for world unification are timeless and will be even more needed in the future than they are today.

The future of Adlerian psychology, then, is bright. Its principles have long found their way into a host of theoretical orientations that give little or no actual recognition to Adler. That may be more frustrating to Adlerians than it would be to Adler himself, who would have undoubtedly been pleased to see some of his ideas that were once seen as radical now becoming universally accepted.

Susan Belangee, a professor and clinician in Georgia, reflected that once upon a time, Adlerians were writing and speaking about how to use Adler's ideas to address any and all syndromes and disorders. She wonders why we don't see very many articles or workshops these days on the "how-to's" when Adler provided such an innovative model with open-forum counseling demonstrations. Perhaps that is something to consider doing. She adds that the mission is to explore and to teach how to use Adlerian theory and techniques with LGBTQ clients. Adler's theory evolved over time where sexual orientation is concerned—he moved from viewing homosexuality as definitively neurotic to a more accepting stance later on, basing his decision on whether the client was happy and productive rather than on sexual orientation alone. Heeding the call to "go beyond Adler," Belangee thinks that her efforts advance Adler's theory where he left off, bringing it into alignment with contemporary practice guidelines on ethical practice. This type of adaptation helps to keep Adlerian theory viable.

During a recent training session on using acceptance and commitment therapy (ACT) to treat eating disorders, Belangee remarked that she found herself "jotting words in the margin of my handout—private logic, fictional finalism, organ inferiority, lifestyle. As the speaker discussed the foundation and strategies for ACT, I found myself feeling pretty justified in how I've been working with my clients. In fact, another article is brewing in my mind—maybe I'll title it 'How ACT confirms Adler'" (S. Belangee, personal communication, July 25, 2015).

Jay Colker, director of the Center for Adlerian Practice and Scholarship at Adler University, reflected on Dreikurs's distinct lines of vertical and horizontal movement. He observed that individuals moving *vertically* are more concerned with personal superiority and prestige. They live with constant tension, fear, and anxieties of falling down, of somehow being "less than." They are vulnerable to criticism from others or themselves and believe that making mistakes or revealing imperfections may lower their status and open them up to ridicule, humiliation, and a conclusion of not being good enough. *Horizontal* movement is quite the opposite—individuals feel accepted, valued, and believe they have a place of significance. They are fully engaged in the tasks of life and are more focused on contributing and adding value than on their status and place in the world. They can forget themselves and look more outwardly rather than inwardly as to whether or not they are good enough. Individuals functioning in this way accept that they are imperfect and see mistakes not as a threat but as a natural part of growth and development. They have what Dreikurs described as the "courage to be imperfect."

Colker believes that the climate today across many cultures is to function vertically. Maybe this is an effort to compensate for feeling "less than" and disenfranchised. Rather than seeking to work with others, many groups of individuals want to be as good as, if not better than, others. Maybe this comes from feeling that privileged individuals remain in denial at best, or at worst are actively maintaining a power position to the detriment of a large class of minorities. It seems as if we are in another cultural revolution. Dreikurs in the 1950s noted a movement from autocratic toward democratic ideals. Colker believes the future of Adlerian psychology is tied to creating a sense of belonging to the larger community. Adlerians must find a way to engage communities in a dialogue that stimulates mutual respect and a sense of belonging to a cause greater than oneself. Colker is not certain how best to accomplish this, but he thinks practicing Adlerians have an obligation to move this agenda forward (J. Colker, personal communication, July 25, 2015).

To understand how to remain relevant, Adlerians need to think of context. There are many issues facing individuals today: economics and environmental concerns, cultural context, gender issues, and generational issues. The Internet is fostering entirely different expectations around engagement. Young people want very much to be at the table, cocreating the world and immediately adding value. If they are not recognized in this way, they turn off and, for example, leave jobs and move on. Colker does not want them leaving Adlerian psychology for a different orientation that appears to be more inclusive. Finally, if Adler or Dreikurs were alive today, Colker wonders if the contextual factors noted above would have them evolving their ideas. Adlerians need to evolve thinking to meet today's challenges, just as Dreikurs did in the past.

James R. Bitter, a professor at East Tennessee University and president-elect of NASAP, states that when Alfred Adler first proposed his model of individual psychology, he intended it to be a comprehensive approach that could be used with all people and genders, multiple cultures, and across the socioeconomic spectrum. He used his model to work with couples, families, and groups, as well as with individuals. This comprehensive model placed a huge emphasis on therapeutic presence, teleological understanding, holistic assessment, and community feeling/social interest as a guiding principle for living effectively and working with clients. Adler, however, could not have known about the advances that would be made in neuropsychology, biology, and genetics, and drugs that would interact with the human mind with the precision of a smart bomb. With the rise of managed care and insurance-based health care, the emphasis on EBP has placed a stronger emphasis on curing a psychological disorder than on understanding the person and helping them reorient to life (J. Bitter, personal communication, August 24, 2015).

The future for Adlerian counseling and psychotherapy depends on the ability of practitioners to bridge Adlerian concepts and practices with the various configurations of mental health delivery across the globe. It differs from country to country, but no model will survive that dismisses the biological in favor of a purely psychological or sociopsychological intervention system. It all has to work together. Bitter believes that one Adlerian who is leading the way in creating this bridge is Paul Rasmussen, a clinical psychologist who works with military personnel who have returned from war zones with both physical and psychological wounds. Rasmussen's (2010) book, *The Quest to Feel Good*, is a must-read for Adlerians. His approach to therapy, currently called *adaptive reorientation therapy*, is a blend of Millon's evolutionary psychology, Adlerian psychology, and cognitive therapy. This model is well on its way to becoming fully integrated into the Veterans Affairs system in South Carolina, and it is the model that will, or at least should, serve as a foundation for Adlerian psychotherapy for the next decade or two.

Richard Watts, past-president of NASAP and professor at Sam Houston State University, states that in the future, when scholars perform due diligence in examining the origins of key ideas in counseling and psychotherapy, they will continue to discover the pioneering work of Alfred Adler and subsequent Adlerians (R. Watts, personal communication, August 11, 2015). Perhaps more than any other theoretical approach, Adlerian therapy allows clinicians to be what Arnold Lazarus (1997) originally called a "therapeutic chameleon." A vital aspect of Adlerian therapy is its integrative flexibility. Adlerian therapists tailor therapy to the unique needs and situations of clients. The Adlerian model allows clinicians to be technically integrative while maintaining theoretical and conceptual consistency; that is, it allows them to be therapeutic chameleons. The field of psychotherapy is catching up with ideas Adler expressed in the mature formulation of his theory. Thus, as the field of counseling and psychotherapy develops, Watts believes it will continue to include Adlerian psychology and practice, and recognition and clinical use of the Adlerian approach to counseling and psychotherapy will increase.

Laurie Sackett-Maniacci, clinical psychologist and faculty member at Adler University, recognizes that the movement to integrate mental health into primary care (and other health care settings) creates opportunities for the use of Adlerian psychology. The holistic approach of Adlerian theory is certainly in line with the integration movement because the integration of mental health and physical wellness is closer to a biopsychosocial model. From both a theoretical and utilization perspective, this would be a natural progression for Adlerians. Adlerians have been conceptualizing health and illness in this way for a long time, allowing for a clear, systematic application of interventions that stem from this framework. Inasmuch as the integration movement would be served by the biopsychosocial approach, it does seem that many of the integrative approaches still work within the biomedical model. (Of course, this could be said for much of the delivery of mental/behavioral health services.) In this way, a true holistic approach will not be undertaken and both the conceptualization and treatment approaches in integrated care may be limited. It is here that Adlerian theory can continue to "fill in the gaps" per se by continuing to introduce and weave Adlerian psychology in these settings, produce research on its utility, or even create new settings where integration of a true holistic model can take hold (L. Sackett-Maniacci, personal communication, August 11, 2015).

Another important area of development speaks to the continued emphasis on the use of evidence-based treatment interventions and EBP. Evidence-based research on Adlerian techniques exists in the Adlerian literature and should continue. In addition, research that looks at how Adlerian interventions and theory can integrate with other evidence-based systems should also continue. In this way we don't have to reinvent the wheel, but can continue to pair Adlerian and other treatments. For example, the lifestyle assessment can contribute a great deal to the identification of core beliefs and schemas seen in cognitive behavioral approaches. Research on the use of mindfulness in targeting the self task (i.e., "learning to be your own best friend") or increasing social interest (i.e., "being present in the moment or practicing loving-kindness") are other examples.

Yet another idea might be to research how certain lifestyles may be more amenable to one approach over another (e.g., traditional cognitive behavior vs. ACT). Where we can quantitatively measure Adlerian concepts and interventions, we should; where we might struggle, perhaps we can also focus research on the interplay of the subjective qualitative nature of Adlerian techniques with the quantitative.

CONCLUSION

This chapter examined future directions for Adlerian psychotherapy. Whereas the Adlerian approach is rich in theory and practical ideas, there is a need for further development in order to advance Adler's theoretical concepts and to match the needs of modern psychotherapy. For example, many Adlerians have been much less focused on outcomes and have been satisfied with anecdotal information on the efficacy of the approaches we have used. There is a need for the Adlerians to engage in research on the work and the interventions used.

7

Summary

You cannot alter facts, but you can alter your way of looking at them.
I have found there is always a less bitter way if you look hard enough.

—Alfred Adler

Adlerian therapy is one of the oldest approaches to psychotherapy. Though the model has shown its longevity, Alfred Adler was also ahead of his time, as he helped create a theory that remains at the forefront of innovative and effective psychotherapy practice. Many of the core components of the approach have been incorporated by the other major theories of today (Corey, 2016). Adler developed his approach in Europe during times of vast social upheaval and ethnic and national conflicts. Being on the receiving end and experiencing marginalization himself, he developed his approach to the notion of unifying humanity and encouraging healthy ways for all people to live together. Foreshadowing the field of positive

http://dx.doi.org/10.1037/0000014-007
Adlerian Psychotherapy, by J. Carlson and M. Englar-Carlson

psychology, Adler stressed that psychologists should help people by focusing on their strengths and assets (Mozdzierz, 2015). Further, Adler advanced the idea that the subjective view of the client was the most important reality to focus upon. He understood that when our thinking is distorted, we make mistakes that prevent us from liking others and ourselves and from finding satisfying work and meaning in life. An overarching tenet of Adlerian psychotherapy is that all people live in a social world in which healthy people contribute to the greater good of all humankind, and each person does so in a unique manner.

CORE CONCEPTS

The Adlerian approach to understanding human behavior integrates thinking, feeling, behaving, and systemic approaches. It is a complete approach that allows for understanding people in the way they want to be understood. People are not divided into component parts but are indivisible and need to be considered holistically. Core beliefs behind Adlerian psychotherapy suggest that people are motivated by social factors; are responsible for their own thoughts, feelings, and actions; are the creators of their own lives (as opposed to being helpless victims); and are driven by purposes and goals, looking more toward the future than back to the past.

The basic goal of the Adlerian approach is to help clients identify and change their mistaken beliefs about self, others, and life, and thus to participate more fully in a social world. Clients are not viewed as psychologically sick, but as discouraged. The therapeutic process helps individuals become aware of their patterns and make basic changes in their style of living, which leads to changes in the way they feel and behave. Adlerians pay special attention to the role of the family development of each person, noting that one's family is the setting in which most patterns of life are established.

Psychotherapy itself is viewed as a cooperative venture that challenges clients to translate their insights into action in the real world. The therapist plays multiple roles, using assessment, psychoeducation, and counseling skills to work with clients to help them meet their goals. Contemporary Adlerian theory can be viewed as an integrative approach, combining cognitive, constructivist, existential, psychodynamic, and systems perspectives. Some of these common characteristics include establishing a respectful client–therapist relationship, emphasizing clients' strengths and resources, understanding the client within the context of their family atmosphere, and holding an optimistic and future orientation.

Adlerians highlight the importance of understanding people within their social context. It is not possible to understand others in isolation, because everything one does pertains to one's social context. Further, an individual's culture helps to create the rules, roles, and outlook that each person must be understood within their cultural context. This understanding will dictate the nature of the intervention. This understanding allows therapists to operate on a variety of levels to create lasting change. The approach is one that shows great respect for all people regardless of gender, ethnicity, race, and sexual orientation. The approach is truly democratic and respects the notion that all people are equal and deserve to be treated in that fashion. Adlerians advocate for social justice and the rights of all people.

One of the strengths of the Adlerian approach is its flexibility and integrative nature. Whereas many modern approaches to psychotherapy can be categorized by an emphasis on one mode, the Adlerian model is holistic, and at its core are a variety of relational, cognitive, behavioral, emotive, systemic, and experiential techniques. Adlerian therapists are resourceful, flexible, and technically eclectic in drawing on many methods that can be applied to a diverse range of clients in a variety of settings and formats. Rather than focusing on fitting clients within one theoretical framework, Adlerians are concerned with doing what is in the best interests of clients (Carlson, Watts, & Maniacci, 2006; Watts & Pietrzak, 2000; Watts & Shulman, 2003).

BRIEF THERAPEUTIC APPROACH

Another contribution of the Adlerian approach is that it is suited to brief, time-limited therapy (Ferrero et al., 2007). Adler was the original proponent of time-limited therapy (Ansbacher, 1972a; Nicoll, Bitter, Christensen, & Hawes, 2000; Slavik, Sperry, & Carlson, 2000; Sperry, 1989), and the techniques used by many contemporary brief therapeutic approaches are very similar to interventions created by or commonly used by Adlerian practitioners (Carlson & Sperry, 2000; Carlson et al., 2006; Wood, 2003). Adlerian therapy and contemporary brief therapy have in common a number of characteristics, including quickly establishing a strong therapeutic alliance, a clear problem focus and goal alignment, rapid assessment and application to treatment, an emphasis on active and directive intervention, a psychoeducational focus, a present and future orientation, a focus on clients' strengths and abilities and an optimistic expectation of change, and a time sensitivity that tailors treatment to the unique needs of the client (Carlson et al., 2006; Hoyt, 2009; Hoyt & Talmon, 2014; Slavik et al., 2000). Early recollections are a significant assessment intervention in brief therapy because they quickly help identify a client's lifestyle and basic mistakes (Mosak & Di Pietro, 2006). Early recollections are often useful in minimizing the number of therapy sessions. This procedure takes very little time to administer and interpret and provides a clear direction for unlocking the core personality of a client.

Bitter and Nicoll (2000) identified five characteristics that form the basis for an integrative framework for Adlerian brief therapy: time limitation, focus, counselor directiveness, symptoms as solutions, and the assignment of behavioral tasks. Bringing a time-limitation process to therapy conveys to clients the expectation that change will occur in a short period of time. When the number of sessions is specified, both client and therapist are motivated to stay focused on desired outcomes and to work as efficiently as possible (Wampold, 2010). Because there is no assurance that a future session will occur, brief therapists tend to ask themselves this question: "If I had only one session to be useful in this person's life, what would I want to accomplish?" (p. 38).

CONTRIBUTION OF THE ADLERIAN APPROACH TO CONTEMPORARY PSYCHOTHERAPY

Adlerian psychology is a phenomenological, holistic, optimistic, and socially embedded theory based on basic assumptions that have been woven into various theories of counseling (Maniacci, Sackett-Maniacci, & Mosak, 2014). Clearly, one of Adler's most important contributions was his influence on other therapy systems. Whereas Freud often overshadows Adler in importance, it is difficult to overestimate the contributions Adler made to contemporary therapeutic practice. In many ways, his influence on current theory and actual practice is greater than Freud's. Many of his ideas were revolutionary and far ahead of his time. Psychology pioneers Abraham Maslow, Viktor Frankl, Rollo May, Paul Watzlawick, Karen Horney, Erich Fromm, Carl Rogers, Virginia Satir, William Glasser, Aaron T. Beck, and Albert Ellis have all acknowledged their debt to Adler.

Many of his core concepts have found their way into most of the other psychological schools, a few of which include existential–humanistic therapy, cognitive behavior therapy, rational emotive behavior therapy, reality therapy, solution-focused brief therapy, and family therapy. In many respects, Adler paved the way for current developments in both the cognitive and constructivist therapies (Watts, 2003, 2012). Adlerians' basic premise is that if clients can change their thinking then they can change their feelings and behavior. Both Frankl and May saw Adler as a forerunner of the existential movement because of his position that human beings are free to choose and are entirely responsible for what they make of themselves (Corey, 2016). This view also makes him a forerunner of the subjective approach to psychology, which focuses on the internal determinants of behavior: values, beliefs, attitudes, goals, interests, personal meanings, subjective perceptions of reality, and strivings toward self-realization.

Adler was keenly aware of the role of context in shaping the lives of people, and the role of sociopolitical factors. He wrote about the influence of discrimination, oppression, poverty, and prejudice on people's psyche and mental health. Bitter (2008) and his colleagues (Bitter, Robertson, Healey, & Jones-Cole, 2009) have drawn attention to the link between Adlerian thinking and feminist therapy approaches. In addition, Adler's influence went beyond counseling individuals, extending into the community mental health movement (Ansbacher, 1972b), child guidance, and schools.

A study of contemporary counseling theories revealed that many of Adler's notions have reappeared in these modern approaches with different nomenclature, and often without giving Adler the credit that is due to him (Watts & Shulman, 2003). One example of this is found in the emergence of the positive psychology movement, which calls for an increased study of hope, courage, contentment, happiness, well-being, perseverance, resilience, tolerance, and personal resources. Adler clearly addressed major themes associated with positive psychology long before this approach appeared on the therapeutic scene (Watts, 2012). It is clear that there are significant linkages between Adlerian theory and most contemporary theories, especially those that view the person as purposive, self-determining, and striving for growth. Carlson and Englar-Carlson (2012) asserted that Adlerians face the challenge of continuing to develop their approach so that it meets the needs of the contemporary global society: "Whereas Adlerian ideas are alive in other theoretical approaches, there is a question about whether Adlerian theory as a stand-alone approach is viable in the long term" (p. 124). With so many Adlerian concepts co-opted by other models, for the Adlerian model to survive and thrive it will be necessary to find ways to strive for its uniqueness and significance.

APPRECIATING THE VISION OF ADLER

Alfred Adler, like Martin Luther King, Jr., had a dream about what life could be about, not a nightmare about what was wrong with the world. He lived in challenging times, not unlike today. Adler offered hope during a time when the world was on a self-destructive path (through World War I and leading up to World War II). He offered specific strategies and paths to follow that would lead to a better life for all people, and because of that, Adler had great popularity. He had a positive vision about what life could be like one day. He tackled society's larger problems and issues, such as gender inequities, power differences, poverty, powerlessness, being disenfranchised, social and relationship skills, and true democratic living. In a September 20, 1925 *New York Times* article, we get a glimpse into the real Adler:

> Individual psychology could rally all the latent forces for good which are inherent in groups, just as it is already rallying such latent forces in individuals. War, national hatreds and class struggle—these greatest enemies of humankind—all root in the desire of groups to escape, or compensate for, the crushing sense of their inferiority. Individual

psychology, which can cure individuals of the evil effects of this sense
of inferiority, might be developed into a most powerful instrument
for ridding nations and groups of the menace of their collective inferiority complexes. . . . . What I said concerning the hatreds and jealou-
sies that urge nations and groups against one another holds also good
for the bitter struggle of the sexes—a struggle that is poisoning love
and marriage and is ever born anew out of the under evaluation of
woman. (Bagger, 1925, p. 12)

Adler himself was more focused on teaching others the basic concepts
of individual psychology rather than formalizing his theoretical approach.
He valued practicing and teaching before organizing and presenting a well-
defined and systematic theory. Adler was a brilliant theoretician, but he was
not scholarly, so he was not able to advance his approach through academic
channels and institution as was the method of formalizing approaches during his lifetime (Engel, 2008). As a result, his written presentations are often
difficult to follow, and many of them are transcripts of lectures he gave. Yet
Adler's global reach was unprecedented. Unfortunately, he became increas-
ingly busy in helping as many people as possible through his clinical work,
demonstrations, and teaching, such that he failed to attend to the work
of those who translated his work (Maniacci, 2012). Over time, prominent Adlerians like Rudolf Dreikurs, Heinz and Rowena Ansbacher, Don
Dinkmeyer, Harold Mosak, Mim Pew, Bernard Shulman, Bob Powers, Jane
Griffiths, Edna Nash, Manford Sonstegard, Jon Carlson, Judy Sutherland,
Julia Yang, Len Sperry, James Bitter, Betty Lou Bettner, Michael Maniacci,
Eva Ferguson Dreikurs, Leigh Johnson-Migalski, Terry Kottman, Roy Kern,
Susan Belangee, Richard Watts, Marion Balla, and Mary Francis Schneider
have helped shape Adler's ideas and vision into a more consistent psycho-
therapeutic approach.

IN CLOSING

The Adlerian model appears almost like a chameleon depending on the
background of the client and the presenting concern. Though Adler was
clearly influential on how others practice contemporary psychotherapy,

some have asked, "So what? Is Adlerian therapy useful for today?" (Watts, 2000b). Our answer to that question is to recognize that much of Adler's original approach to human behavior has been co-opted by other approaches and actually represents the contemporary delivery of mental health services and supports. We wonder how effective psychotherapy services could be if more therapists used a complete approach rather than just the pieces or segments that seemed to work. Utilizing Adler's vision from assessment to conceptualization to treatment and then termination might result in even deeper and more impactful psychotherapy services.

Adlerian psychotherapy is a psychoeducational, present-future-oriented, and time-limited (or brief) approach. In addition, Adlerian therapy, albeit theoretically consistent, is both integrative and eclectic, clearly integrates cognitive and systemic perspectives, and solidly resonates with postmodern approaches (Watts, 2000b). If you are confused or uncertain about some of the ideas contained in this book in the Theories of Psychotherapy Series, be assured that they will come up again in the guise of the other theories in the series that have taken the concepts and developed them further. Adlerian psychotherapy was not only the first truly integrative helping system, but it remains one of the truly holistic integrated systems of psychotherapy.

Appendix:
Lifestyle Questionnaire Inventory

DIRECTIONS*

Below is a list of brothers and sisters, starting with the oldest.

	Age
1. older brother	17
2. older sister	14
3. me (male)	12
4. younger brother	8
5. youngest sister	6

You notice the descending order is numbered beginning with 1 (older brother), and ending with 5 (youngest sister). The numbers will be used to rate brothers and sisters on a particular item.

Example:
Helping around the house

     most __2__ more __3__ average ____ less __1__ least __5__

    In this example the older sister is most helpful. You do not help as much, but you are more helpful than your older brother and youngest sister.

This is not a test. There are no "right" or "wrong" answers. Take as much time as you need; answer as fairly as you are able.

Turn to Part 1. At the top of the page make a list of your brothers and sisters, starting with the oldest. Give their ages. Be sure to include yourself by indicating "me." Please identify which sex.

_____

_____

_____

Designed by Roy Kern

* If you are an only child, do not complete this questionnaire.

Part I

Now make your list according to the directions given.

Age   Age

1. _____   4. _____

2. _____   5. _____

3. _____   6. _____

Using the birth-order number (1, 2, 3, etc.) rate each family member on the traits listed below. Imagine that you are 12 years old when making comparisons.

Intelligence   most_____ more_____ average_____ less_____ least_____

Hardest   most_____ more_____ average_____ less_____ least_____
  worker

Best grades   most_____ more_____ average_____ less_____ least_____
  in school

Helping around the house	most____	more____	average____	less____	least____
Obedient	most____	more____	average____	less____	least____
Rebellious	most____	more____	average____	less____	least____
Trying to please	most____	more____	average____	less____	least____
Critical of others	most____	more____	average____	less____	least____
Considerate	most____	more____	average____	less____	least____
Selfish	most____	more____	average____	less____	least____
Having own way	most____	more____	average____	less____	least____
Sensitive— easily hurt	most____	more____	average____	less____	least____
Temper tantrum	most____	more____	average____	less____	least____
Highest aspiration	most____	more____	average____	less____	least____
Materialistic	most____	more____	average____	less____	least____
Desire to excel	most____	more____	average____	less____	least____
Good behavior	most____	more____	average____	less____	least____
Athletic	most____	more____	average____	less____	least____
Spoiled	most____	more____	average____	less____	least____
Punished	most____	more____	average____	less____	least____

Part II

Continue to use the numbers in answering the following questions. Space is provided for brief comments.

1. Among your brothers and sisters, who is most different from you?

   _____

   In what way?

   _____

   _____

   _____

2. Who is most like you? _____

   In what way?

   _____

   _____

   _____

3. Which of you has the most friends? _____

4. Who is your father's favorite? _____

5. Who is your mother's favorite? _____

6. Which two fight and argue the most? _____

7. Which two play together most? _____

8. What kind of person was your father?

   _____

   _____

   _____

9. What kind of person was your mother?

   _____

   _____

   _____

10. Who were you most like? _____

In what ways?

_____

_____

_____

Part III

Give a brief description of yourself:

_____

_____

_____

Part IV

Try to remember your earliest recollections. Please provide at least three different ones from under the age of 8. Include as many details as you can as well as your <u>reactions</u> and <u>feelings</u>. Make sure that it is a recollection you remember and not information someone in your family has reported to you.

Example: I was 5 years of age, and I remember throwing my older brother down to the floor. I felt strong, proud, and powerful.

ER 1._____

_____

_____

ER 2._____

_____

_____

ER 3._____

_____

_____

Glossary of Key Terms

BASIC MISTAKES   Self-defeating aspects of a person's lifestyle that include perceptions, attitudes, and beliefs. They may have been useful at one time, but they often have negative effects on later behavior. These mistakes can include denying one's worth, overgeneralizations, faulty values, setting impossible-to-reach goals, having an exaggerated need for security, a need to seek power, or avoidance of others.

DISCOURAGEMENT   Lacking courage; the opposite of encouragement, when people feel they do not belong in a useful, constructive manner.

EARLY RECOLLECTIONS   A single incident an individual can recall that occurred before the age of 8; it must be able to be visualized, have a narrative (even if sparse), and should have a feeling associated with it and a part that vividly stands out.

ENCOURAGEMENT   This is a therapy technique for building the therapy relationship and fostering client change. Encouragement is the process of helping clients to feel they have worth as they are. It is shown when therapists demonstrate social interest to and for their clients. It can help increase one's courage to face life tasks.

FAMILY CONSTELLATION   The early developmental influences upon a person, typically comprising siblings, parents, other key persons, and the neighborhood and community. It includes an emphasis on birth order, as well as the personality characteristics of members of the family that influence sibling and parental relationships. Family constellation helps determine lifestyle.

FAULTY LOGIC   Convictions that run counter to social interest; convictions that are unique to the individual and do not facilitate useful, constructive belonging.

HOLISM   Understanding people as integrated beings with a focus on how the person moves through life and how all of the parts of a person fit together.

INFERIORITY   A feeling or appraisal of deficiency that is subjective, global, and judgmental. Often developed during early childhood and serves as the basis to strive for superiority to overcoming feelings of being "less than."

INFERIORITY COMPLEX   A behavioral manifestation of a subjective belief or feeling of inferiority. It is usually a strong and exaggerated sense that one is not as good as other people.

LIFE GOALS   Goals that individuals select that are beneficial to others; they do not interfere with others. Example: Striving to be excellent at a task as opposed to being better than others.

LIFESTYLE   The attitudes and convictions people have about how to find their place in the world; the instructions for how to belong.

LIFE TASKS   Adler originally defined three (work, love, and community) universal tasks that represent the main challenges people experience in life. All three must be addressed in order to function effectively.

MISTAKEN GOALS   Goals that are detrimental to others, such as those that run counter to social interest. Example: Wanting to be better than others as opposed to helpful to others.

PRIVATE LOGIC   Ideas conceived in childhood that comprise one's deeply established personal beliefs or constructs.

SELF-CONCEPT   The sum of all of the convictions and attitudes individuals have about themselves that can complete either of two sentences: "I am . . ." or "I am not . . ." For example, "I am a winner," "I am tall," "I am a slow learner." Often learned through mirroring with caregivers and actual experience with life.

SELF-IDEAL   Ideals about what should be about the world and people. Self-ideals include all of the convictions and attitudes that people have about themselves that can complete either of the following two sentences: "In order to belong, I should . . ." or "In order to find my place, I should not . . ."

SOCIAL INTEREST   An interest in the interests of others. Behaviors and attitudes that display a sense of fellow feeling, responsibility, and community with others, not just for today but for generations yet to come.

Suggested Readings
and Resources

ADLERIAN PROFESSIONAL ORGANIZATION

North American Society of Adlerian Psychology (NASAP) is the primary organization in the United States for the promotion of the psychological and philosophical theories of individual psychology. NASAP was founded in 1952 and has a broad spectrum of professional members in the fields of education, psychology, psychiatry, counseling, social work, pastoral care, business, and family education.

NASAP
429 E. Dupont Road #276
Ft. Wayne, IN 46825
http://www.alfredadler.org

PROFESSIONAL JOURNALS

The Journal of Individual Psychology is the journal of NASAP and follows the natural evolution of two earlier journals, *The Individual Psychologist* and *Individual Psychology*. As the premier scholarly forum for Adlerian practices, principles, and theoretical development, *The Journal of Individual Psychology* also addresses techniques, skills, and strategies associated with the practice and application of Adlerian psychological methods (see http://www.utexas.edu/utpress/journals/jip.html).

> The journal is also available from NASAP or the
> University of Texas Press
> P.O. Box 7819
> Austin, TX 78713-7819
> 1-800-252-3206
> http://www.utpress.utexas.edu/

Dialoghi Adleriani is an online journal that is produced twice per year by the Alfred Adler Institute of Milan, Italy. It was founded in 2014 by the Editor-in-Chief Giuseppe Ferrigno. The journal was created for members of the helping professions and offers a wide variety of articles in English and Italian. The publication is in an electronic format and is free of charge. The publication welcomes Adlerian as well as other orientations with the goal of encouraging "dialogue." (Back issues are also available online [http://www.scuolaadleriana.it/index.php/rivista] by entering "Archivo riviste.")

ADLERPEDIA (ADLERIAN ONLINE ENCYCLOPEDIA)

AdlerPedia is a comprehensive website (http://www.adler.org) for everything Adlerian created by Jay Colker and Jon Carlson at Adler University, Chicago. AdlerPedia is open to anyone without restrictions. Access information on over 80 basic Adlerian concepts including definitions, articles, videos available for streaming, and handouts. Other professionals can be contacted and engaged in discussions by practice area. There are case conceptualization materials and video discussions on cases presented by students and others. Learn about Adler's influence on many of the contemporary philosophies of psychology. Read about contemporary Adlerians as well as many of the pioneers. Access additional materials related to these Adlerians as well. Finally, link to Adlerian organizations and businesses.

ADLERIAN YEARBOOKS

Each year since 1996, the Adlerian Society UK publishes a yearbook containing a collection of topical essays pertaining to individual psychology. Each issue aims to provide a diverse range of practice-based, theoretical, and historical contributions by contributors from the United Kingdom, Canada, Israel, Switzerland, and the United States. The yearbooks and other publications are available online (see http://www.adleriansociety.co.uk/).

ADLERIAN UNIVERSITIES AND TRAINING CENTERS

NASAP has a list of the 58 Adlerian organizations and institutes (see http://www.alfredadler.org/links).

The Adler University, with campuses in Chicago and Vancouver, offers fully accredited master's and doctoral degree programs:

Adler University
17 North Dearborn Street
Chicago, IL 60602
312-662-4000

Adler University
1090 W. Georgia Street
Suite 1200
Vancouver, BC V6E 3V7
604-482-5510
http://www.adler.edu

The Adler Graduate School, located in Minneapolis, offers fully accredited master's degree programs:

Adler Graduate School
1550 E. 78th Street
Minneapolis, MN 55423
612-861-7554
http://www.alfredadler.edu

SUGGESTED READINGS

Ansbacher, H. L., & Ansbacher, R. R. (Eds.). (1956). *The individual psychology of Alfred Adler: A systematic presentation in selections from his writings.* New York, NY: Harper Torchbooks.
This has been the main source of Adler's writings. The editors' comments are very helpful in understanding Adler's theory and practice.

Carlson, J. D., & Maniacci, M. (2012). *Alfred Adler revisited.* New York, NY: Routledge.
Some of Adler's most important writings placed into contemporary contexts by many of today's leading Adlerian scholars and practitioners.

Carlson, J. D., & Slavik, S. (1997). *Techniques in Adlerian psychology.* Philadelphia, PA: Taylor and Francis.
A collection of classic articles from *The Journal of Individual Psychology* that focus on techniques and practice.

Carlson, J. D., Watts, R. E., & Maniacci, M. (2005). *Adlerian psychotherapy.* Washington, DC: American Psychological Association.
An important book on contemporary Adlerian psychotherapy that provides additional details about the Adlerian approach.

Clark, A. J. (2002). *Early recollections: Theory and practice of counseling and psychotherapy.* New York, NY: Routledge.
Detailed guidelines for how to administer and interpret early recollections.

Dinkmeyer, D., Jr., Carlson, J. D., & Michel, R. (2016). *Consultation: Creating school based interventions* (3rd ed.). New York, NY: Routledge.
A book on how to use Adlerian psychology to work effectively with teachers, parents, and schools.

Dinkmeyer, D., Jr., & Sperry, L. (2000). *Counseling and psychotherapy: An integrated, individual psychology approach.* Columbus, OH: Merrill.
A good basic text on Adlerian counseling and psychotherapy.

Dreikurs, R., & Stoltz, V. (1964). *Children: The challenge.* New York, NY: Hawthorn.
This is the classic text on the Adlerian perspective on parenting and raising a child.

Hoffman, E. (1994). *The drive for self: Alfred Adler and the founding of individual psychology.* Reading, MA: Addison Wesley.
The best biography on the life of Alfred Adler.

Hooper, A., & Holford, J. (1998). *Adler for beginners.* New York, NY: Writers and Readers.
A fun and easy-to-read primer about the life and contributions of Alfred Adler that uses graphics and comics to review the theory.

Kottman, T., & Meany-Walen, K. (2016). *Partners play: An Adlerian approach to play therapy* (3rd ed.). Alexandria, VA: American Counseling Association.
How to integrate Adlerian techniques into play therapy.

Manaster, G. J., & Corsini, R. J. (1982). *Individual psychology: Theory and practice.* Chicago, IL: Adler School of Professional Psychology.
A textbook on individual psychology.

Mosak, H., & Maniacci, M. (1999). *A primer of Adlerian psychology: The analytic–behavioral–cognitive psychology of Alfred Adler.* New York, NY: Brunner-Routledge.
A good source about the "nuts and bolts" of Adlerian psychology.

Mosak, H. H., & Di Pietro, R. (2006). *Early recollections: Interpretative method and application.* New York, NY: Routledge.
A comprehensive textbook on using this important Adlerian projective procedure.

Powers, R. L., & Griffith, J. (2012). *The key to psychotherapy: Understanding the self-created individual* (2nd ed.). Port Townsend, WA: Adlerian Associates.
A manual for how to conduct Adlerian psychotherapy.

Slavik, S., & Carlson, J. D. (2005). *Readings in the theory of Adlerian psychology.* New York, NY: Routledge.
A basic book that contains the major articles that developed the theory of Adlerian psychology.

Sonstegard, M. A., Bitter, J. R., & Pelonis, P. (2004). *Adlerian group counseling and therapy: Step-by-step.* New York, NY: Routledge.
A practical guidebook for learning the Adlerian group therapy process.

Sperry, L., Carlson, J. D., Sauerheber, J., & Sperry, J. (2015). *Psychopathology and psychotherapy: DSM–5 diagnosis, case conceptualization, and treatment* (3rd ed.). New York, NY: Routledge.
How *DSM–5* disorders are treated from an Adlerian perspective.

DEMONSTRATION VIDEOS

Alexander Street Press. (Producer). (2003). *Brief integrative Adlerian couples therapy* [DVD]. Available from http://search.alexanderstreet.com/preview/work/1778761?ssotoken=anonymous
Dr. Jon D. Carlson works with a couple with problems of anger and abuse.

Allyn & Bacon. (Producer). (1998). *Adlerian family therapy* (Series: Family therapy with the experts) [DVD]. Available from http://www.psychotherapy.net/video/adlerian-family-therapy
Dr. James Bitter demonstrates Adlerian family therapy with a mother, father, and their three young children.

Allyn & Bacon. (Producer). (1998). *Adlerian psychotherapy* (Series: Psychotherapy with the experts) [DVD]. Available from http://www.psychotherapy.net/video/adlerian-therapy

Dr. Jon D. Carlson works with an African American woman struggling with her divorce and overfunctioning approach to life.

Allyn & Bacon. (Producer). (2002). *Adlerian parent consultation* (Series: Child therapy with the experts) [DVD]. Available from http://www.psychotherapy.net/video/adlerian-parent-consultation

Dr. Jon D. Carlson provides an example of an individual parent consultation with a single mother and a parent group consultation.

Allyn & Bacon. (Producer). (2002). *Adlerian play therapy* (Series: Child therapy with the experts) [DVD]. Available from http://www.psychotherapy.net/video/adlerian-play-therapy

Dr. Terrry Kottman demonstrates Adlerian play therapy with a 4-year-old boy.

American Psychological Association. (Producer). (2005). *Adlerian therapy* (Series I: Systems of psychotherapy) [DVD]. Available from http://www.apa.org/pubs/videos/4310721.aspx

Dr. Jon D. Carlson works with a young man with issues of perfectionism. In a brief 45-minute session significant change occurred.

American Psychological Association. (Producer). (2006). *Psychotherapy over time* (Series VIII: Psychotherapy in six sessions) [DVD]. Available from http://www.apa.org/pubs/videos/4310745.aspx

Dr. Carlson works with a 30-year-old woman over six sessions to deal with problems of PTSD, depression, substance abuse, anxiety, and personality disorder.

DATABASES

Dr. Harold H. Mosak and Birdie Mosak have created a comprehensive bibliography (http://www.adlerbiblio.com/) for Adlerian psychology.

The Adlerian Digitization Project (http://www.adlerjournals.com/) was created to make available full-text digital copies of early issues of *The Journal of Individual Psychology*, *The Individual Psychologist*, and other difficult-to-obtain books and journals.

References

Adler, A. (1917). *Study of organ inferiority and its psychical compensation: A contribution to clinical medicine.* http://dx.doi.org/10.1037/10734-000

Adler, A. (1927a). The cause and prevention of neuroses. *Journal of Mental Science, 73*, 1–8.

Adler, A. (1927b). *The practice and theory of individual psychology.* New York, NY: Harcourt Brace.

Adler, A. (1927c). *Understanding human nature.* Garden City, NY: Garden City.

Adler, A. (1929). Advice for the consultant. *Internationale Zeitschrift für Individualpsychologie, 7*, 202–203.

Adler, A. (1935). What is neurosis? *International Journal of Individual Psychology, 1*, 9–17.

Adler, A. (1938). *Social interest: A challenge to mankind.* London, England: Faber and Faber.

Adler, A. (1956). Organ dialect. In H. L. Ansbacher & R. R. Ansbacher (Eds.), *The individual psychology of Alfred Adler: A systematic presentation in selections from his writings* (pp. 222–227). New York, NY: Basic Books.

Adler, A. (1979). *Superiority and social interest: A collection of later writings* (3rd ed.) New York, NY: Norton.

Adler, A. (1992). *What life could mean to you* (C. Brett, Trans.). Oxford, England: Oneworld. (Original work published 1931)

Adler, K. (1994). Foreword. In E. Hoffman (Ed.), *The drive for self: Alfred Adler and the founding of individual psychology* (p. xii). New York, NY: Addison-Wesley.

Alizadeh, H. (2012). Individual psychology and Islam: An exploration of social interest. *The Journal of Individual Psychology, 68*, 216–224.

Ansbacher, H. L. (1972a). Adlerian psychotherapy: The tradition of brief psychotherapy. *Individual Psychology: Journal of Adlerian Theory, Research & Practice, 28*, 137–151.

Ansbacher, H. L. (1972b). Goal oriented individual psychology: Alfred Adler's theory. In A. Burton (Ed.), *Operational theories of personality* (pp. 99–142). New York, NY: Brunner/Mazel.

Ansbacher, H. L. (1983). Individual psychology. In R. J. Corsini & A. J. Marsella (Eds.), *Personality theories, research, and assessment* (pp. 69–123). Itasca, IL: Peacock.

Ansbacher, H. L. (1991). The development of Adler's concept of social interest: A critical study. *Individual Psychology: Journal of Adlerian Theory, Research & Practice, 47*, 64–65.

Ansbacher, H. L. (1992a). Alfred Adler, pioneer in prevention of mental disorders. *Individual Psychology: Journal of Adlerian Theory, Research & Practice, 48*, 3–34.

Ansbacher, H. L. (1992b). Alfred Adler's concept of community feeling and of social interest and the relevance of community feeling for old age. *Individual Psychology: Journal of Adlerian Theory, Research & Practice, 48*, 402–412.

Ansbacher, H. L., & Ansbacher, R. R. (Eds.). (1956). *The individual psychology of Alfred Adler: A systematic presentation in selections from his writings.* New York, NY: Harper Torchbooks.

Ansbacher, H. L., & Ansbacher, R. R. (Eds. & Trans.). (1978). *Alfred Adler: Cooperation between the sexes: Writings on women and men, love and marriage, and sexuality.* Garden City, NY: Anchor Books.

Arciniega, G. M., Anderson, T. C., Tovar-Blank, Z. G., & Tracey, T. J. G. (2008). Toward a fuller conception of machismo: Development of a traditional machismo and caballerismo scale. *Journal of Counseling Psychology, 55*, 19–33. http://dx.doi.org/10.1037/0022-0167.55.1.19

Arciniega, G. M., & Newlon, B. J. (1999). Counseling and psychotherapy: Multicultural considerations. In D. Capuzzi & D. R. Gross (Eds.), *Counseling & psychotherapy: Theories and interventions* (2nd ed., pp. 435–458). Upper Saddle River, NJ: Merrill/Prentice-Hall.

Bagger, E. (1925, September 25). Inferiority sense held to be our chief enemy: Dr. Adler, founder of "Individual Psychology," claims war can be eliminated and love problems solved by attacking this foe—at variance with Freud. *The New York Times.* Retrieved from http://www.nytimes.com

Balla, M. (2003). Raissa Epstein Adler: Socialist, activist, feminist—1873–1962. In Adlerian Society of the United Kingdom and The Institute for Individual Psychology (Eds.), *Adlerian yearbook, 2003* (pp. 50–58). Wiltshire, England: Anthony Rowe.

Bankart, C. P. (1997). *Talking cures: A history of Western and Eastern psychotherapies.* Pacific Grove, CA: Brooks/Cole.

Baruth, L. G., & Manning, M. L. (1987). God, religion, and the life tasks. *Individual Psychology: Journal of Adlerian Theory, Research & Practice, 43,* 429–436.

Bass, M. L., Curlette, W. L., Kern, R. M., & McWilliams, A. E., Jr. (2002). Social interest: A meta-analysis of a multidimensional construct. *The Journal of Individual Psychology, 58,* 4–34.

Bazzano, M. (2008). When Rogers met Adler: Notes on power, masculinity, and gender in person-centered therapy. *Adlerian Yearbook, 2007,* 125–135.

Bickhard, M., & Ford, B. (1991). Adler's concept of social interest: A critical explication. *Individual Psychology: Journal of Adlerian Theory, Research & Practice, 47,* 61–63.

Bitter, J. R. (2008). Reconsidering narcissism: An Adlerian-feminist response to the articles in the special section of *The Journal of Individual Psychology,* Volume 63, Issue 2. *The Journal of Individual Psychology, 64,* 270–279.

Bitter, J. R. (2013). *Theory and practice of family therapy and counseling* (2nd ed.). Belmont, CA: Brooks Cole.

Bitter, J. R., & Nicoll, W. G. (2000). Adlerian brief therapy with individuals: Process and practice. *The Journal of Individual Psychology, 56,* 31–44.

Bitter, J. R., Robertson, P. E., Healey, A. C., & Jones-Cole, L. K. (2009). Reclaiming a profeminist orientation in Adlerian therapy. *The Journal of Individual Psychology, 65,* 13–33.

Bottome, P. (1939). *Alfred Adler: Apostle of freedom.* New York, NY: G. P. Putnam's.

Boyd-Franklin, N. (1989). Five key factors in the treatment of Black families. *Journal of Psychotherapy & the Family, 6,* 53–69.

Brack, G., Hill, M. B., Edwards, D., Grootboom, N., & Lassiter, P. S. (2003). Adler and Ubuntu: Using Adlerian principles in the New South Africa. *The Journal of Individual Psychology, 59,* 316–326.

Bridge, D. J., & Voss, J. L. (2014). Hippocampal binding of novel information with dominant memory traces can support both memory stability and change. *The Journal of Neuroscience, 34,* 2203–2213. http://dx.doi.org/10.1523/JNEUROSCI.3819-13.2014

Carey, T. A., & Mullan, R. J. (2004). What is Socratic questioning? *Psychotherapy: Theory, Research, Practice, Training, 41,* 217–226. http://dx.doi.org/10.1037/0033-3204.41.3.217

Carlson, J. D. (1989). On beyond Adler. *Individual Psychology: The Journal of Adlerian Theory, Research & Practice, 45,* 411–413.

Carlson, J. D. (2000). Individual psychology in the year 2000 and beyond: Astronaut or dinosaur? Headline or footnote? *The Journal of Individual Psychology, 56,* 3–13.

Carlson, J. D. (2015a). 100 years of psychotherapy. *New Therapist, 100,* 22–25.

Carlson, J. D. (2015b). *Meditation and mindfulness* (NASAP Tap Talk). Retrieved from https://nasap.memberclicks.net/assets/media/TAPTALKS/jon%20carlson%20mindfulness.mp3

Carlson, J. D., & Dinkmeyer, D. C., Jr. (2003). *Time for a better marriage.* Atascadero, CA: Impact.

Carlson, J. D., & Englar-Carlson, M. (2012). Adlerian therapy. In J. Frew & M. Spiegler (Eds.), *Contemporary psychotherapies for a diverse world* (1st ed. rev., pp. 87–130). New York, NY: Routledge.

Carlson, J. D., Englar-Carlson, M., & Emavardhana, T. (2011). Was Adler from Bangkok? Applying an Adlerian/Buddhist approach in Thailand. *The Journal of Individual Psychology, 67,* 349–363.

Carlson, J. D., Englar-Carlson, M., & Emavardhana, T. (2012). Individual psychology in Thailand. *The Journal of Individual Psychology, 68,* 397–410.

Carlson, J. D., & Johnson, J. (2009). Adlerian therapy. In I. Marini & M. A. Stebnicki (Eds.), *The professional counselor's desk reference* (pp. 371–377). New York, NY: Springer.

Carlson, J. D., & Lorelle, S. (2016a). Daily dialogue. In G. Weeks, S. Fife, & C. Peterson (Eds.), *Techniques for the couple's therapist: Essential interventions* (pp. 62–66). New York, NY: Routledge.

Carlson, J. D., & Lorelle, S. (2016b). Taking ownership. In G. Weeks, S. Fife, & C. Peterson (Eds.), *Techniques for the couple's therapist: Essential interventions* (pp. 83–86). New York, NY: Routledge.

Carlson, J. D., & Slavik, S. (1997). *Techniques in Adlerian psychology.* Philadelphia, PA: Taylor & Francis.

Carlson, J. D., & Sperry, L. (1998). Adlerian psychotherapy as a constructivist psychotherapy. In M. F. Hoyt (Ed.), *The handbook of constructive therapies: Innovative approaches from leading practitioners* (pp. 68–82). San Francisco, CA: Jossey-Bass.

Carlson, J. D., & Sperry, L. (2000). *Brief therapy with individuals and couples.* Phoenix, AZ: Zeig, Tucker & Theisen.

Carlson, J. D., Watts, R. E., & Maniacci, M. (2006). *Adlerian psychotherapy.* Washington, DC: American Psychological Association.

Carlson, J. M., & Carlson, J. D. (2000). The application of Adlerian psychotherapy with Asian Americans. *The Journal of Individual Psychology, 56,* 214–225.

Carns, M. R., & Carns, A. W. (2006). A review of the professional literature concerning the consistency of the definition and application of Adlerian encouragement. In S. Slavik & J. Carlson (Eds.), *Readings in the theory of individual psychology* (pp. 277–293). New York, NY: Taylor & Francis.

Chandler, C. K. (1995). Contemporary Adlerian reflections on homosexuality and bisexuality. *Individual Psychology: The Journal of Adlerian Theory, Research & Practice, 51*, 82–89.

Chaplin, M. P., & Orlofsky, J. L. (1991). Personality characteristics of male alcoholics as revealed through their early recollections. *Individual Psychology: The Journal of Adlerian Theory, Research & Practice, 47*, 356–371.

Cheston, S. E. (2000). The spirituality of encouragement. *The Journal of Individual Psychology, 56*, 296–303.

Chung, R. C., & Bemak, F. (1998). Lifestyle of Vietnamese refugee women. *The Journal of Individual Psychology, 54*, 373–384.

Clark, A. J. (2002). *Early recollections: Theory and practice of counseling and psychotherapy.* New York, NY: Routledge.

Clark, A. J. (2007). *Empathy in counseling psychotherapy: Perspectives and practices.* Mahwah, NJ: Erlbaum.

Clark, A. J. (2013). *Dawn of memories: The meaning of early recollections.* New York, NY: Rowman & Littlefield.

Close, R. E. (2015). Adlerian counseling in a virtual world: Some implications of internet practice for the development of *Gemeinschaftsgefühl. The Journal of Individual Psychology, 71*, 155–162. http://dx.doi.org/10.1353/jip.2015.0017

Comas-Díaz, L. (2014). Multicultural psychotherapy. In F. T. L. Leong, L. Comas-Díaz, G. C. Nagayama Hall, V. C. McLoyd, & J. E. Trimble (Eds.), *APA handbook of multicultural psychology: Vol. 2. Applications and training* (pp. 419–441). http://dx.doi.org/10.1037/14187-024

Connor, D. R., & Callahan, J. L. (2015). Impact of psychotherapist expectations on client outcomes. *Psychotherapy, 52*, 351–362. http://dx.doi.org/10.1037/a0038890

Conoley, C. W., Pontrelli, M. E., Oromendia, M. F., Carmen Bello, B. D., & Nagata, C. M. (2015). Positive empathy: A therapeutic skill inspired by positive psychology. *Journal of Clinical Psychology, 71*, 575–583. http://dx.doi.org/10.1002/jclp.22175

Constantino, M. J., Arnkoff, D. B., Glass, C. R., Ametrano, R. M., & Smith, J. Z. (2011). Expectations. *Journal of Clinical Psychology, 67*, 184–192. http://dx.doi.org/10.1002/jclp.20754

Corey, G. (2016). *Theory and practice of counseling and psychotherapy* (10th ed.). Belmont, CA: Brooks-Cole.

Crandall, J. (1984). Social interest as a moderator of life stress. *Journal of Personality and Social Psychology, 47*, 164–174. http://dx.doi.org/10.1037/0022-3514.47.1.164

Curlette, W. L., Wheeler, M. S., & Kern, R. M. (1993). *Basis-A Inventory technical manual.* Highlands, NC: TRT.

Dagley, J. C. (2000). Adlerian family therapy. In A. M. Horne (Ed.), *Family counseling and therapy* (3rd ed., pp. 366–419). Itasca, IL: Peacock.

Daugherty, D. A., Murphy, M. J., & Paugh, J. (2001). An examination of the Adlerian construct of social interest with criminal offenders. *Journal of Counseling & Development, 79*, 465–479.

Debb, S. M., & Blitz, D. L. (2010). Relating ethnic differences and quality of life assessment to individual psychology through the biopsychosocial model. *The Journal of Individual Psychology, 66*, 270–289.

DeRobertis, E. (2011). Deriving a third force approach to child development from the works of Alfred Adler. *Journal of Humanistic Psychology, 51*, 492–515. http://dx.doi.org/10.1177/0022167810386960

Dinkmeyer, D. C., Dinkmeyer, D. C., Jr., & Sperry, L. (1987). *Adlerian counseling and psychotherapy* (2nd ed.). Columbus, OH: Merrill.

Dinkmeyer, D. C., & Dreikurs, R. (1963). *Encouraging children to learn.* Englewood Cliffs, NJ: Prentice-Hall.

Dinkmeyer, D. C., & Losoncy, L. E. (1980). *The encouragement book: Becoming a positive person.* Englewood Cliffs, NJ: Prentice-Hall.

Dinkmeyer, D. C., & Losoncy, L. E. (1996). *The skills of encouragement: Bringing out the best in yourself and others.* Delray Beach, FL: St. Lucie Press.

Dinkmeyer, D. C., Sr., McKay, G. D., & Dinkmeyer, D. C., Jr. (2008). *The parent's handbook.* Circle Pines, MN: American Guidance Service.

Dinkmeyer, D. C., Jr., & Sperry, L. (2000). *Counseling and psychotherapy: An integrated, individual psychology approach* (3rd ed.). Upper Saddle River, NJ: Merrill/Prentice Hall.

Dreikurs, R. (1958). *Psychology in the classroom.* New York, NY: Harper.

Dreikurs, R. (1967). *Psychodynamics, psychotherapy, and counseling.* Chicago, IL: Alfred Adler Institute.

Dreikurs, R. (1971). *Social equality: The challenge of today.* Chicago, IL: Regnery.

Dreikurs, R. (1973). *Psychodynamics, psychotherapy, and counseling: Collected papers* (Rev. Ed.). Chicago, IL: Alfred Adler Institute.

Dreikurs, R., & Cassell, P. (1972). *Discipline without tears.* New York, NY: Penguin.

Dreikurs, R., & Mosak, H. H. (1967). The tasks of life: II. The fourth task. *The Individual Psychologist, 4*, 51–55.

Dreikurs, R., & Soltz, V. (1964). *Children: The challenge.* New York, NY: Hawthorn Books.

Dufrene, R. L. (2011). Adlerian theory. In D. Capuzzi & D. R. Gross (Eds.), *Counseling and psychotherapy* (5th ed., pp. 95–118). Alexandria, VA: American Counseling Association.

Eckstein, D., Aycock, K. J., Sperber, M. A., McDonald, J., Van Wiesner, V. I., Watts, R. E., & Ginsburg, P. (2010). A review of 200 birth-order studies: Lifestyle characteristics. *The Journal of Individual Psychology, 66,* 408–434.

Eckstein, D., & Cooke, P. (2005). The seven methods of encouragement for couples. *The Family Journal, 13,* 342–350. http://dx.doi.org/10.1177/1066480705276384

Eckstein, D., & Kaufman, J. A. (2012). The role of birth order in personality: An enduring intellectual legacy of Alfred Adler. *The Journal of Individual Psychology, 68,* 60–61.

Ecrement, E. R., & Zarski, J. J. (1987). The pastor-as-counselor: Adlerian contributions to the process. *Individual Psychology: The Journal of Adlerian Theory, Research & Practice, 43,* 461–467.

Edwards, D. J., Gfroerer, K., Flowers, C., & Whitaker, Y. (2004). The relationship between social interest and coping resources in children. *Professional School Counseling, 7,* 187–194.

Ellenberger, H. F. (1981). *The discovery of the unconscious: The history and evolution of dynamic psychiatry* (Rev. ed.). New York, NY: Basic Books.

Ellis, A. (2000). Spiritual goals and spirited values in psychotherapy. *Individual Psychology: The Journal of Adlerian Theory, Research & Practice, 56,* 277–284.

Engel, J. (2008). *American therapy: The rise of psychotherapy in the United States.* New York, NY: Gotham Books.

Ergüner-Tekinalp, B., & Terzi, S. (2014). Coping, social interest, and psychological birth order as predictors of resilience in Turkey. *Applied Research in Quality of Life, 2,* 509–524. http://dx.doi.org/10.1007/s11482-014-9378-3

Erickson, R. C. (1984). Social interest: Relating Adlerian psychology to Christian theology. *Pastoral Psychology, 32,* 131–139. http://dx.doi.org/10.1007/BF01082956

Evans, T. D. (1996). Encouragement: The key to reforming classrooms. *Educational Leadership, 54,* 81–85.

Evans, T. D., Dedrick, R. F., & Epstein, M. J. (1997). Development and initial validation of the encouragement scale (educator form). *The Journal of Humanistic Education and Development, 35,* 163–174. http://dx.doi.org/10.1002/j.2164-4683.1997.tb00366.x

Falicov, C. J. (2010). Changing constructions of machismo for Latino men in therapy: "The devil never sleeps." *Family Process, 49,* 309–329. http://dx.doi.org/10.1111/j.1545-5300.2010.01325.x

Falicov, C. J. (2014). *Latino families in therapy* (2nd ed.). New York, NY: Guilford.

Ferguson, E. D. (2001). Adler and Dreikurs: Cognitive-social dynamic innovators. *The Journal of Individual Psychology, 57,* 324–341.

Ferguson, E. D. (2015). Alfred Adler's profound understanding of social motivation. *The General Psychologist, 49,* 18–20.

Ferrero, A. (2012). The model of sequential brief-Adlerian psychodynamic psychotherapy (SB-APP): Specific features in the treatment of borderline personality disorder. *Ricerca In Psicoterapia/Research In Psychotherapy: Psychopathology, Process and Outcome, 15,* 32–45.

Ferrero, A., Pierò, A., Fassina, S., Massola, T., Lanteri, A., Daga, G. A., & Fassino, S. (2007). A 12-month comparison of brief psychodynamic psychotherapy and pharmacotherapy treatment in subjects with generalised anxiety disorders in a community setting. *European Psychiatry, 22,* 530–539. http://dx.doi.org/10.1016/j.eurpsy.2007.07.004

Fiebert, M. (1997). In and out of Freud's shadow: A chronology of Adler's relationship with Freud. *Individual Psychology: The Journal of Adlerian Theory, Research & Practice, 53,* 241–269.

Frevert, V. S., & Miranda, A. O. (1998). A conceptual formulation of the Latin culture and the treatment of Latinos from an Adlerian psychology perspective. *The Journal of Individual Psychology, 54,* 291–309.

Gallagher, P. E. (1998). Review of the BASIS–A Inventory (Basic Adlerian Scales for Interpersonal Success—Adult Form). In J. C. Impara & L. L. Murphy (Eds.), *The thirteenth mental measurements yearbook* (pp. 81–82). Lincoln, NE: Buros Institute.

Gilbert, D. (2006). *Stumbling on happiness.* New York, NY: Knopf.

Gilman, R. (2001). The relationship between life satisfaction, social interest, and frequency of extracurricular activities among adolescent students. *Journal of Youth and Adolescence, 30,* 749–767. http://dx.doi.org/10.1023/A:1012285729701

Giordano, A. L., & Cashwell, C. S. (2014). Exploring the relationship between social interest, social bonding, and collegiate substance abuse. *Journal of College Counseling, 17,* 222–235. http://dx.doi.org/10.1002/j.2161-1882.2014.00059.x

Giordano, A. L., Clarke, P. B., & Furter, R. T. (2014). Predicting substance abuse relapse: The role of social interest and social bonding. *Journal of Addictions & Offender Counseling, 35,* 114–127. http://dx.doi.org/10.1002/j.2161-1874.2014.00030.x

Glass, J., & Owen, J. (2010). Latino fathers: The relationship among machismo, acculturation, ethnic identity, and paternal involvement. *Psychology of Men & Masculinity, 11,* 251–261. http://dx.doi.org/10.1037/a0021477

Goleman, D. (2015). *A force for good: The Dalai Lama's vision for our world.* New York, NY: Bantam.

Griffith, J. (2006). Adler's organ jargon. In S. Slavik & J. D. Carlson (Eds.), *Readings in the theory of individual psychology* (pp. 83–90). New York, NY: Taylor & Francis.

Griffith, J., & Powers, R. L. (2007). *The lexicon of Adlerian psychology* (2nd ed.). Port Townsend, WA: Adlerian Psychology Associates.

Hammond, H. (2015). Social interest, empathy, and online support groups. *The Journal of Individual Psychology, 71*, 174–184. http://dx.doi.org/10.1353/jip.2015.0008

Handlbauer, B. (1998). *The Freud-Adler controversy.* Oxford, England: Oneworld.

Hanna, F. J. (1996). Community feeling, empathy, and intersubjectivity: A phenomenological framework. *The Journal of Individual Psychology, 52*, 22–30.

Hanna, F. J. (1998). A transcultural view of prejudice, racism, and community feeling: The desire and striving for status. *The Journal of Individual Psychology, 54*, 336–345.

Hartshorne, J. K., Salem-Hartshorne, N., & Hartshorne, T. S. (2009). Birth order effects in the formation of long-term relationships. *The Journal of Individual Psychology, 65*, 156–176.

Hays, P. (2009). Integrating evidence-based practice, cognitive–behavior therapy, and multicultural therapy: Ten steps for culturally competent practice. *Professional Psychology: Research and Practice, 40*, 354–360. http://dx.doi.org/10.1037/a0016250

Heiland, F. (2009). Does the birth order affect the cognitive development of a child? *Applied Economics, 41*, 1799–1818. http://dx.doi.org/10.1080/00036840601083220

Hendrix, H., Hunt, H. L. K., Luquet, W., & Carlson, J. (2015). Using the Imago dialogue to deepen couple's therapy. *The Journal of Individual Psychology, 71*, 253–272. http://dx.doi.org/10.1353/jip.2015.0029

Herring, R. D., & Runion, K. B. (1994). Counseling ethnic children and youth from an Adlerian perspective. *Journal of Multicultural Counseling and Development, 22*, 215–226. http://dx.doi.org/10.1002/j.2161-1912.1994.tb00255.x

Hoffman, E. (1994). *The drive for self: Alfred Adler and the founding of individual psychology.* Reading, MA: Addison Wesley.

Hoyt, M. F. (2009). *Brief psychotherapies: Principles and practices.* Phoenix, AZ: Zeig, Tucker & Theisen.

Hoyt, M. F., & Talmon, M. (2014). *Capturing the moment: Single session therapy and walk-in services.* Bristol, CT: Crown House.

Huber, R. J. (1991). On beyond Adler and anamnesis. *Individual Psychology: Journal of Adlerian Theory, Research & Practice, 47*, 433–436.

Johansen, T. M. (2005). Applying individual psychology to work with clients of the Islamic faith. *The Journal of Individual Psychology, 61*, 174–184.

Johnson, P., Smith, A. J., & Nelson, M. D. (2003). Predictors of social interest in young adults. *The Journal of Individual Psychology, 59,* 281–292.

Jones, S. L., & Butman, R. E. (1991). *Modern psychotherapies: A comprehensive Christian appraisal.* Downers Grove, IL: Inter Varsity Press Academic.

Jones-Smith, E. (2012). *Theories of counseling and psychotherapy: An integrative approach.* Thousand Oaks, CA: Sage.

Kanz, J. E. (2001). The applicability of individual psychology for work with conservative Christian clients. *The Journal of Individual Psychology, 57,* 342–353.

Kawulich, B. B., & Curlette, W. L. (1998). Life tasks and the Native American perspectives. *The Journal of Individual Psychology, 54,* 359–367.

Kelly, F. D. (2002). The effects of locus of control, gender, and grade upon children's preference for praise or encouragement. *The Journal of Individual Psychology, 58,* 197–207.

Kelly, F. D., & Daniels, J. G. (1997). The effects of praise versus encouragement on children's perceptions of teachers. *Individual Psychology: Journal of Adlerian Theory, Research & Practice, 53,* 331–341.

Kern, R., Gfroerer, K., Summers, Y., Curlette, W., & Matheny, K. (1996). Lifestyle, personality, and stress coping. *Individual Psychology: Journal of Adlerian Theory, Research & Practice, 52,* 42–53.

Kim, E., & Hogge, I. (2013). An Adlerian conceptualization of Korean women with hwa-byung. *The Journal of Individual Psychology, 69,* 41–54.

Kim, E., Park, H. J., & Hogge, I. (2015). Examination of the Adlerian constructs of activity and social interest with depression among recent Korean retirees: Meaning in life as a mediator. *Archives of Gerontology and Geriatrics, 61,* 378–383. http://dx.doi.org/10.1016/j.archger.2015.07.003

King, R., & Shelley, C. (2008). Community feeling and social interest: Adlerian parallels, synergy and differences with the field of community psychology. *Journal of Community & Applied Social Psychology, 18,* 96–107. http://dx.doi.org/10.1002/casp.962

Kottler, J. A. (2002). *Theories in counseling and therapy: An experiential approach.* Boston, MA: Allyn & Bacon.

Kottler, J. A., Englar-Carlson, M., & Carlson, J. D. (Eds.). (2013). *Helping beyond the 50-minute hour: Therapists engaged in social action.* New York, NY: Routledge.

Kottman, T. (2011). *Play therapy: Basics and beyond* (2nd ed.). Alexandria, VA: American Counseling Association.

Kottman, T., & Ashby, J. (2015). Adlerian play therapy. In D. Crenshaw & A. Stewart (Eds.), *Play therapy: A comprehensive guide to theory and practice* (pp. 32–47). New York, NY: Guilford Press.

Kottman, T., & Meany-Walen, K. (2016). *Partners play: An Adlerian approach to play therapy* (3rd ed.). Alexandria, VA: American Counseling Association.

Lambert, M. J. (2013). The efficacy and effectiveness of psychotherapy. In M. Lambert (Ed.), *Handbook of psychotherapy and behavior change* (6th ed., pp. 169–218). New York, NY: Wiley and Sons.

Lambert, S. F., LeBlanc, M., Mullen, J. A., Ray, D., Baggerly, J., White, J., & Kaplan, D. (2007). Learning more about those who play in session: The National Play Therapy in Counseling Practices Project (Phase 1). *Journal of Counseling & Development, 85,* 42–46. http://dx.doi.org/10.1002/j.1556-6678.2007.tb00442.x

La Roche, M., & Christopher, M. (2009). Changing paradigms from empirically supported treatment to evidence-based practice: A cultural perspective. *Professional Psychology: Research and Practice, 40,* 396–402. http://dx.doi.org/10.1037/a0015240

Lazarus, A. A. (1997). *Brief but comprehensive psychotherapy: The multimodal way.* New York, NY: Springer.

Leak, G. K., & Leak, K. C. (2006). Adlerian social interest and positive psychology: A conceptual and empirical integration. *The Journal of Individual Psychology, 62,* 207–223.

Leak, G. K., & Williams, D. (1991). Relationship between social interest and perceived family environment. *Individual Psychology: Journal of Adlerian Theory, Research & Practice, 47,* 159–165.

Lewis, T. F., & Watts, R. E. (2004). The predictability of Adlerian lifestyle themes compared to demographic variables associated with college student drinking. *The Journal of Individual Psychology, 60,* 245–264.

Lindquist, T., & Watkins, K. (2014). Modern approaches to modern challenges: A review of widely used parenting programs. *The Journal of Individual Psychology, 70,* 148–165. http://dx.doi.org/10.1353/jip.2014.0013

Love, P., & Carlson, J. D. (2011). *Never be lonely again: The way out of emptiness, isolation and a life unfulfilled.* New York, NY: HCI Books.

Luborsky, L., Rosenthal, R., Diguer, L., Andrusyna, T. P., Berman, J. S., Levitt, J. T., . . . Krause, E. D. (2002). The dodo bird verdict is alive and well—Mostly. *Clinical Psychology: Science and Practice, 9,* 2–12. http://dx.doi.org/10.1093/clipsy.9.1.2

Main, F. O., & Boughner, S. R. (2011). Encouragement and actionable hope: The source of Adler's clinical agency. *The Journal of Individual Psychology, 67,* 269–291.

Manaster, G. J., & Corsini, R. J. (1982). *Individual psychology: Theory and practice.* Chicago, IL: Adler School of Professional Psychology.

Maniacci, M. (2012). An introduction to Alfred Adler. In J. Carlson & M. Maniacci (Eds.), *Alfred Adler revisited* (pp. 1–10). New York, NY: Routledge.

Maniacci, M. P., Sackett-Maniacci, L., & Mosak, H. H. (2014). Adlerian psychotherapy. In D. Wedding & R. J. Corsini (Eds.), *Current psychotherapies* (10th ed., pp. 55–94). Belmont, CA: Cengage Learning.

Mansager, E. (2000). Individual psychology and the study of spirituality. *The Journal of Individual Psychology, 56*, 371–388.

Mansager, E., Cold, L., Griffith, B., Kai, E., Manaster, G., McArter, G., . . . Silverman, N. N. (2002). Spirituality in the Adlerian forum. *The Journal of Individual Psychology, 58*, 177–196.

Matteson, D. R. (1995). Counseling with bisexuals. *Individual Psychology: Journal of Adlerian Theory, Research & Practice, 51*, 144–159.

McBrien, R. J. (2004). Expanding social interest through forgiveness. *The Journal of Individual Psychology, 60*, 408–419.

McGoldrick, M., Giordano, J., & Garcia-Preto, N. (2005). Overview: Ethnicity and family therapy. In M. McGoldrick, J. Giordano, & N. Garcia-Preto (Eds.), *Ethnicity and family therapy* (3rd ed., pp. 1–40). New York, NY: Guilford Press.

McKay, G. D. (2012). Position in family constellation influences lifestyle. In J. D. Carlson & M. Maniacci (Eds.), *Alfred Adler revisited* (pp. 71–88). New York, NY: Routledge.

Meany-Walen, K. K., Bratton, S. C., & Kottman, T. (2014). Effects of Adlerian play therapy on reducing students' disruptive behaviors. *Journal of Counseling & Development, 92*, 47–56. http://dx.doi.org/10.1002/j.1556-6676.2014.00129.x

Meany-Walen, K. K., Bullis, Q., Kottman, T., & Dillman Taylor, D. (2015). Group Adlerian play therapy with children with off-task behaviors. *Journal for Specialists in Group Work, 40*, 294–314. http://dx.doi.org/10.1080/01933922.2015.1056569

Meany-Walen, K. K., Kottman, T., Bullis, Q., & Dillman Taylor, D. (2015). Effects of Adlerian play therapy on children's externalizing behavior. *Journal of Counseling & Development, 93*, 418–428. http://dx.doi.org/10.1002/jcad.12040

Meunier, G. F. (1989). Encouragement groups with nursing-home elderly. *Individual Psychology: Journal of Adlerian Theory, Research & Practice, 45*, 459–464.

Miller, S., Wampold, B., & Varhely, K. (2008). Direct comparisons of treatment modalities for youth disorders: A meta-analysis. *Psychotherapy Research, 18*, 5–14. http://dx.doi.org/10.1080/10503300701472131

Milliren, A. P., & Clemmer, F. (2006). Introduction to Adlerian psychology: Basic principles and methodology. In S. Slavik & J. D. Carlson (Eds.), *Readings in the theory of individual psychology* (pp. 17–32). New York, NY: Routledge.

Milliren, A. P., Evans, T. D., & Newbauer, J. F. (2007). Adlerian theory. In D. Capuzzi & D. R. Gross (Eds.), *Counseling and psychotherapy: Theories and interventions* (4th ed., pp. 123–163). Upper Saddle River, NJ: Merrill Prentice-Hall.

Mills, K. J., & Mooney, G. A. (2013). Methods of ranking birth order: The neglected issue in birth order research. *The Journal of Individual Psychology, 69*, 357–370.

Miranda, A. O., & Fraser, L. D. (2002). Culture-bound syndromes: Initial perspectives from individual psychology. *The Journal of Individual Psychology, 58*, 422–433.

Miranda, A. O., Frevert, V. S., & Kern, R. M. (1998). Lifestyle differences between bicultural, and low and high acculturation level Latinos. *Individual Psychology: Journal of Adlerian Theory, Research & Practice, 54*, 119–134.

Moore, N., & McDowell, T. (2014). Expanding Adlerian application: The tasks, challenges, and obstacles for African American parents. *The Journal of Individual Psychology, 70*, 114–127. http://dx.doi.org/10.1353/jip.2014.0011

Mosak, H. H. (1989). Adlerian psychotherapy. In R. J. Corsini & D. Wedding (Eds.), *Current psychotherapies* (4th ed., pp. 64–116). Itasca, IL: Peacock.

Mosak, H. H. (2005). Adlerian psychotherapy. In R. J. Corsini & D. Wedding (Eds.), *Current psychotherapies* (7th ed., pp. 52–95). Belmont, CA: Brooks/Cole.

Mosak, H. H., & Di Pietro, R. (2006). *Early recollections: Interpretative method and application.* New York, NY: Routledge.

Mosak, H. H., & Maniacci, M. P. (1998). *Tactics in counseling and psychotherapy.* Itasca, IL: F.E. Peacock.

Mosak, H. H., & Maniacci, M. P. (1999). *A primer of Adlerian psychology: The analytic–behavioral–cognitive psychology of Alfred Adler.* Philadelphia, PA: Taylor & Francis.

Mozdzierz, G. J. (2015). Pragmatics and operational principles of positive psychology research and clinical findings with implications for Adlerian psychology. *The Journal of Individual Psychology, 71*, 362–398. http://dx.doi.org/10.1353/jip.2015.0033

Mozdzierz, G. J., Greenblatt, R. L., & Murphy, T. J. (2007). The measurement and clinical use of social interest: Validation of the Sulliman Scale of Social Interest on a sample of hospitalized substance abuse patients. *The Journal of Individual Psychology, 63*, 225–234.

Mozdzierz, G. J., & Krauss, H. H. (1996). The embeddedness of Alfred Adler in modern psychology: Social policy and planning implications. *Individual Psychology: Journal of Adlerian Theory, Research & Practice, 52*, 224–236.

Nicoll, W. G., Bitter, J. R., Christensen, O. C., & Hawes, C. (2000). Adlerian brief therapy: Strategies and tactics. In J. D. Carlson & L. Sperry (Eds.), *Brief therapy with individuals and couples* (pp. 220–247). Phoenix, AZ: Zeig, Tucker & Theisen.

Nietzsche, F. (1888). *Twilight of idols.* London, England: Oxford University Press.

Nikelly, A., & Dinkmeyer, D. (1971). *Techniques for behavior change: Applications of Adlerian theory.* Springfield, IL: Charles C Thomas.

Noda, S. J. (2000). The concept of holism in individual psychology and Buddhism. *The Journal of Individual Psychology, 56,* 285–295.

Norcross, J. C. (Ed.). (2002). *Psychotherapy relationships that work: Therapist contributions and responsiveness to patient needs.* New York, NY: Oxford University Press.

Norcross, J. C., Hedges, M., & Prochaska, J. O. (2002). The face of 2010: A Delphi poll on the future of psychotherapy. *Professional Psychology: Research and Practice, 33,* 316–322. http://dx.doi.org/10.1037/0735-7028.33.3.316

Norcross, J. C., Krebs, P. M., & Prochaska, J. O. (2011). Stages of change. *Journal of Clinical Psychology, 67,* 143–154. http://dx.doi.org/10.1002/jclp.20758

Orgler, H. (1963). *Alfred Adler: The man and his works: Triumph over the inferiority complex.* New York, NY: Mentor Books. (Original work published in 1939)

Overholser, J. C. (2010). Psychotherapy that strives to encourage social interest: A simulated interview with Alfred Adler. *Journal of Psychotherapy Integration, 20,* 347–363. http://dx.doi.org/10.1037/a0022033

Parham, T. A. (2002). Counseling African Americans: The current state of affairs. In T. A. Parham (Ed.), *Counseling persons of African descent: Raising the bar of practitioner competence* (pp. 1–9). http://dx.doi.org/10.4135/9781452229119.n1

Pedrotti, J. T. (2011). Broadening perspectives: Strategies to infuse multiculturalism into a positive psychology course. *The Journal of Positive Psychology, 6,* 506–513. http://dx.doi.org/10.1080/17439760.2011.634817

Pedrotti, J. T., Edwards, L. M., & Lopez, S. (2009). Positive psychology within a cultural context. In S. Lopez & C. Snyder (Eds.), *The Oxford handbook of positive psychology* (2nd ed., pp. 49–57). New York, NY: Oxford University Press.

Peluso, P. R. (2012). Personality as a self-consistent unity: A contemporary view. In J. D. Carlson & M. Maniacci (Eds.), *Alfred Adler revisited* (pp. 57–70). New York, NY: Routledge.

Perkins-Dock, R. E. (2005). The application of Adlerian family therapy with African American families. *The Journal of Individual Psychology, 61,* 233–249.

Pety, J., Kelly, F. D., & Kafafy, A. E. (1984). The Praise–Encouragement Preference scale for children. *Individual Psychology: Journal of Adlerian Theory, Research & Practice, 40,* 92–101.

Phelps, R. E., Tranakos-Howe, S., Dagley, J. C., & Lyn, M. K. (2001). Encouragement and ethnicity in African American college students. *Journal of Counseling & Development, 79,* 90–97. http://dx.doi.org/10.1002/j.1556-6676.2001.tb01947.x

Phillips, F. B. (1990). NTU psychotherapy: An Afrocentric approach. *Journal of Black Psychology, 17,* 55–74. http://dx.doi.org/10.1177/00957984900171005

Powers, R. L., & Griffith, J. (1987). *Understanding lifestyle: The psycho-clarity process.* Port Townsend, WA: Adlerian Psychology Associates.

Prochaska, J. O., & Norcross, J. C. (2010). *Systems of psychotherapy* (7th ed.). Belmont, CA: Brooks/Cole.

Prochaska, J. O., Norcross, J. C., & DiClemente, C. C. (2007). *Changing for good: A revolutionary six-stage program for overcoming bad habits and moving your life positively forward.* New York, NY: William Morrow.

Pryor, D. B., & Tollerud, T. R. (1999). Applications of Adlerian principles in school settings. *Professional School Counseling, 2,* 299–304.

Rasmussen, P. R. (2010). *The quest to feel good.* New York, NY: Routledge/Taylor & Francis Group.

Ratts, M. J., Singh, A. A., Nassar-McMillan, S. C., Butler, S. K., & McCullough, J. R. (2016). Multicultural and social justice counseling competencies: Guidelines for the counseling profession. *Journal of Multicultural Counseling and Development, 44,* 28–48. http://dx.doi.org/10.1002/jmcd.12035

Reddy, I., & Hanna, F. J. (1995). The lifestyle of the Hindu woman: Conceptualizing female clients of Indian origin. *The Journal of Individual Psychology, 51,* 216–230.

Roberts, R. L., Harper, R., Caldwell, R., & Decora, M. (2003). Adlerian lifestyle analysis of Lakota women: Implications for counseling. *The Journal of Individual Psychology, 59,* 15–29.

Roberts, R. L., Harper, R., Tuttle Eagle Bull, D., & Heideman-Provost, L. M. (1998). The Native American medicine wheel and individual psychology: Common themes. *The Journal of Individual Psychology, 54,* 135–145.

Rogers, C. (1961). *On becoming a person.* Boston, MA: Houghton Mifflin.

Rowles, J., & Duan, C. (2012). Perceived racism and encouragement among African American adults. *Journal of Multicultural Counseling and Development, 40,* 11–23. http://dx.doi.org/10.1111/j.2161-1912.2012.00002.x

Rubel, D. J., & Ratts, M. J. (2011). Diversity and social justice issues in counseling and psychotherapy. In D. Capuzzi & D. R. Gross (Eds.), *Counseling and psychotherapy* (5th ed., pp. 29–51). Alexandria, VA: American Counseling Association.

Santiago-Valles, W. F. (2009). Social interest: Context and impact of Raissa Epstein's ideas on Alfred Adler's social imaginary (1897–1935). *The Journal of Individual Psychology, 65,* 360–379.

Sapp, M. (2006). The strength-based model for counseling at-risk youths. *The Counseling Psychologist, 34,* 108–117. http://dx.doi.org/10.1177/0011000005282370

Sapp, M. (2014). Adlerian counseling and hypnosis: Strategies for African American adolescents. *Australian Journal of Clinical Hypnotherapy and Hypnosis, 36,* 37–46.

Sauerheber, J. D., & Bitter, J. R. (2013). An Adlerian approach in premarital counseling with religious couples. *The Journal of Individual Psychology, 69,* 305–327.

Shelley, C. (2009). Trans people and social justice. *The Journal of Individual Psychology, 65,* 386–396.

Shifron, R. (2010). Adler's need to belong as the key for mental health. *The Journal of Individual Psychology, 66,* 10–29.

Shulman, B. H. (1973). *Contributions to individual psychology.* Chicago, IL: Alfred Adler Institute.

Shulman, B. H., & Mosak, H. H. (1977). Birth order and ordinal position: Two Adlerian views. *Journal of Individual Psychology, 33,* 114–121.

Shulman, B. H., & Mosak, H. H. (1988). *Manual for life style assessment.* Muncie, IN: Accelerated Development.

Slavik, S., & Carlson, J. D. (2006). *Readings in the theory of individual psychology.* New York, NY: Taylor & Francis.

Slavik, S., Sperry, L., & Carlson, J. D. (2000). Efficient Adlerian therapy with individuals and couples. In J. D. Carlson & L. Sperry (Eds.), *Brief therapy with individuals and couples* (pp. 248–263). Phoenix, AZ: Zeig, Tucker & Theisen.

Smith, T. B., Rodríguez, M. D., & Bernal, G. (2011). Culture. *Journal of Clinical Psychology, 67,* 166–175. http://dx.doi.org/10.1002/jclp.20757

Sonstegard, M. A., Bitter, J. R., & Pelonis, P. (2004). *Adlerian group counseling and therapy: Step-by-step.* New York, NY: Routledge.

Sperry, L. (1989). Special issue: Varieties of brief therapy. *Individual Psychology: Journal of Adlerian Theory, Research & Practice, 45,* 1–2.

Sperry, L. (1991). An alternative future for individual psychology: A challenging agenda for NASAP. *Individual Psychology: Journal of Adlerian Theory, Research & Practice, 47,* 548–553.

Sperry, L. (2011). Core competencies and competence-based Adlerian psychotherapy. *The Journal of Individual Psychology, 67,* 380–390.

Sperry, L. (2015). Diagnosis, case conceptualization, culture, and treatment. In L. Sperry, J. Carlson, J. D. Sauerheber, & J. Sperry (Eds.), *Psychopathology and psychotherapy: DSM–5 diagnosis, case conceptualization, and treatment* (3rd ed., pp. 1–14). New York, NY: Routledge.

Sperry, L. (2016a). Educating the next generation of psychotherapists: Considering the future of theory and practice in Adlerian Psychotherapy. *The Journal of Individual Psychology, 72,* 4–11.

Sperry, L. (2016b). *Handbook of diagnosis and treatment of DSM–5 personality disorders* (3rd ed.). New York, NY: Routledge.

Sperry, L., & Carlson, J. (2012a). Continuing our global look at individual psychology. *The Journal of Individual Psychology, 68*, 309.

Sperry, L., & Carlson, J. (2012b). The global significance of individual psychology: An introduction and overview. *The Journal of Individual Psychology, 68*, 205–209.

Sperry, L., & Carlson, J. D. (2013). *How master therapists work: Effecting change from first through the last session and beyond.* New York, NY: Routledge.

Sperry, L., Carlson, J. D., Sauerheber, J., & Sperry, J. (2015). *Psychopathology and psychotherapy: DSM–5 diagnosis, case conceptualization, and treatment* (3rd ed.). New York, NY: Routledge.

Stein, H. T. (1991). Adler and Socrates: Similarities and differences. *Individual Psychology: Journal of Adlerian Theory, Research & Practice, 47*, 241–246.

Stein, H. T. (2013). *Classical Adlerian depth psychotherapy: Vol. 1. Theory and practice: A Socratic approach.* Bellingham: Adler Institute of Northwestern Washington.

Stein, H. T., & Edwards, M. E. (1998). Alfred Adler: Classical theory and practice. In P. Marcus & A. Rosenberg (Eds.), *Psychoanalytic versions of the human condition: Philosophies of life and their impact on practice* (pp. 64–93). New York, NY: New York University Press.

Stewart, A. E. (2012). Issues in birth order research methodology: Perspectives from individual psychology. *The Journal of Individual Psychology, 68*, 75–106.

Sue, S., & Zane, N. (1987). The role of culture and cultural techniques in psychotherapy. A critique and reformulation. *American Psychologist, 42*, 37–45. http://dx.doi.org/10.1037/0003-066X.42.1.37

Sun, S., & Bitter, J. R. (2012). From China to South Korea: Two perspectives on individual psychology in Asia. *The Journal of Individual Psychology, 68*, 233–248.

Suprina, J. S., Brack, C. J., Chang, C. Y., & Kim, J. (2010). Differences of lifestyle and coping resources between gay men with and without alcohol problems. *The Journal of Individual Psychology, 66*, 166–187.

Sweeney, T. J. (2009). *Adlerian counseling and psychotherapy: A practitioner's approach.* New York, NY: Taylor & Francis.

Uccello, C. (2009). Social interest and social responsibility in contemporary corporate environments. *The Journal of Individual Psychology, 65*, 412–419.

Vaihinger, H. (1924). *The philosophy of "as if": A system of the theoretical, practical and religious fictions of mankind.* London, England: Routledge & Kegan Paul.

Wampold, B. E. (2010). *The basics of psychotherapy: An introduction to theory and practice.* Washington, DC: American Psychological Association.

Wampold, B. E., & Imel, Z. E. (2015). *The great psychotherapy debate: The evidence for what makes psychotherapy work* (2nd ed.). New York, NY: Routledge.

Watkins, C. E. (1997). An Adlerian reaction in the spirit of social interest: Dialogue worth reckoning with. *Journal of Cognitive Psychotherapy, 11*, 211–214.

Watkins, C. E., & Blazina, C. (1994). Reliability of the Sulliman Scale of Social Interest. *Individual Psychology: Journal of Adlerian Theory, Research & Practice, 50*, 164–165.

Watts, R. E. (1998). The remarkable similarity between Rogers' core conditions and Adler's social interest. *The Journal of Individual Psychology, 54*, 4–9.

Watts, R. E. (2000a). Biblically based Christian spirituality and Adlerian psychotherapy. *The Journal of Individual Psychology, 56*, 316–328.

Watts, R. E. (2000b). Entering the new millennium: Is individual psychology still relevant? *The Journal of Individual Psychology, 56*, 21–30.

Watts, R. E. (Ed.). (2003). *Adlerian, cognitive, and constructivist psychotherapies: An integrative dialogue.* New York, NY: Springer.

Watts, R. E. (2012). On the origin of the striving for superiority and of social interest (1933). In J. D. Carlson & M. Maniacci (Eds.), *Alfred Adler revisited* (pp. 41–46). New York, NY: Routledge.

Watts, R. E., & Carlson, J. D. (Eds.). (1999). *Interventions and strategies in counseling and psychotherapy.* Philadelphia, PA: Taylor & Francis.

Watts, R. E., & Critelli, J. W. (1997). Roots of contemporary cognitive theories in the individual psychology of Alfred Adler. *Journal of Cognitive Psychotherapy, 11*, 147–156.

Watts, R. E., & LaGuardia, A. C. (2015, March). *Being a therapeutic chameleon: Integrative Adlerian procedures and techniques for effective brief counseling.* Presented at the American Counseling Association World Conference, Orlando, FL.

Watts, R. E., Peluso, P. R., & Lewis, T. F. (2005). Expanding the acting as if technique: An Adlerian/constructive integration. *The Journal of Individual Psychology, 61*, 380–387.

Watts, R. E., & Phillips, K. A. (2004). Adlerian psychology and psychotherapy: A relational constructivist approach. In J. D. Raskin & S. K. Bridges (Eds.), *Studies in meaning 2: Bridging the personal and social in constructivist psychology* (pp. 267–289). New York, NY: Pace University Press.

Watts, R. E., & Pietrzak, D. (2000). Adlerian "encouragement" and the therapeutic process of solution-focused brief therapy. *Journal of Counseling & Development, 78*, 442–447. http://dx.doi.org/10.1002/j.1556-6676.2000.tb01927.x

Watts, R. E., & Shulman, B. H. (2003). Integrating Adlerian and constructive psychotherapies: An Adlerian perspective. In R. E. Watts (Ed.), *Adlerian, cognitive and constructivist theories of counseling and psychotherapy: An integrative dialogue* (pp. 9–37). New York, NY: Springer.

Westen, D., Novotny, C. M., & Thompson-Brenner, H. (2005). EBP ≠ EST: Reply to Crits-Christoph et al. (2005) and Weisz et al. (2005). *Psychological Bulletin, 131,* 427–433. http://dx.doi.org/10.1037/0033-2909.131.3.427

Whaley, A. L., & Davis, K. E. (2007). Cultural competence and evidence-based practice in mental health services: A complementary perspective. *American Psychologist, 62,* 563–574. http://dx.doi.org/10.1037/0003-066X.62.6.563

Williams, C. B. (2005). Counseling African American women: Multiple identities—multiple constraints. *Journal of Counseling & Development, 83,* 278–283. http://dx.doi.org/10.1002/j.1556-6678.2005.tb00343.x

Wong, Y. J. (2015). The psychology of encouragement: Theory, research, and applications. *The Counseling Psychologist, 43,* 178–216. http://dx.doi.org/10.1177/0011000014545091

Wood, A. (2003). Alfred Adler's treatment as a form of brief therapy. *Journal of Contemporary Psychotherapy, 33,* 287–301. http://dx.doi.org/10.1023/B:JOCP.0000004500.47149.8d

Yang, J., & Milliren, A. (2009). *The psychology of courage: An Adlerian handbook for healthy social living.* New York, NY: Routledge.

Index

About the Authors

Jon Carlson, PsyD, EdD, ABPP, is the Distinguished Professor of Adlerian Psychology at Adler University, Chicago, and a psychologist with the Wellness Clinic in Lake Geneva, Wisconsin. Dr. Carlson is also Professor Emeritus at Governors State University in the Division of Psychology and Counseling, University Park, Illinois. He is a fellow of the American Psychological Association, the American Counseling Association, and the Wisconsin Psychology Association. Dr. Carlson has written 62 books and over 180 articles and book chapters, and created over 300 professional training videos that are being used in universities and training centers around the world. Five of the videos and seven of the books are on Adlerian psychotherapy. He has served as the editor of several periodicals, including *The Journal of Individual Psychology* and *The Family Journal.* He holds diplomates in both family psychology and Adlerian psychology, received a Certificate of Psychotherapy from the Alfred Adler Institute (now Adler University), and received the Lifetime Contribution Award from NASAP (North American Society of Adlerian Psychology). He received the Distinguished Psychologist Award (lifetime contribution to psychotherapy, APA Division 29: Society for the Advancement of Psychotherapy) and the 2011 Distinguished Career Contributions to Education and Training Award from the American Psychological Association.

Matt Englar-Carlson, PhD, is a professor of counseling and the director of the Center for Boys and Men at California State University–Fullerton. He is a fellow of the American Psychological Association (Division 51: Society for the Psychological Study of Men and Masculinity). He was raised Adlerian and is interested in promoting culturally responsive Adlerian practice. As a scholar, teacher, and clinician, Dr. Englar-Carlson is focused on training clinicians to work more effectively with their male clients across the full range of human diversity. He has over 40 publications and 65 national and international presentations, most of which are focused on men and masculinity, social justice, diversity issues in psychological training and practice, and on theories of psychotherapy. Dr. Englar-Carlson coedited the books *In the Room With Men: A Casebook of Therapeutic Change, Counseling Troubled Boys: A Guidebook for Professionals, Beyond the 50-Minute Hour: Therapists Involved in Meaningful Social Action*, and *A Counselor's Guide to Working With Men*, and was featured in the APA-produced DVD *Engaging Men in Psychotherapy*. He was named the Researcher of the Year and Professional of the Year by the Society for the Psychological Study of Men and Masculinity. As a clinician, he has worked with children, adults, and families in school, community, and university mental health settings.